SUR/PETITION

*Creating Value Monopolies
When Everyo...
Me...*

Edward de Bono

HarperBusiness
A Division of HarperCollins*Publishers*

A hardcover edition of this book was published in 1992 by HarperBusiness, a division of HarperCollins Publishers.

HarperCollins books may be purchased for educational, business, or sales promotional use. For information please write: Special Markets Department, HarperCollins Publishers, Inc., 10 East 53rd Street, New York, NY 10022.

First paperback edition published 1993.

The Library of Congress has catalogued the hardcover edition as follows:
De Bono, Edward, 1933–
    Sur/petition : creating value monopolies when everyone else is merely competing / by Edward de Bono.
    p.   cm.
    Includes index.
    ISBN 0-88730-543-1
    1. Creative ability in business.   2. Competition.   I. Title.
HD53.D4   1992
650.1–dc20   91-42190

ISBN 0-88730-599-7 (pbk.)
93 94 95 96 97 RRD 10 9 8 7 6 5 4 3 2 1

Contents

Introduction

In this book I wish to show that the notion of competition is a dangerous and seductive trap that limits and restricts business thinking. Anyone involved in running a business needs to move beyond competition to *sur/petition*.

Competition is a fashionable concept vigorously pushed by such gurus as Michael Porter of the Harvard Business School. But any business school has to be about ten years behind the times in its thinking in order to be credible. This is true because its ideas have to be immediately acceptable; since there is a considerable time lag, the ideas of the future are not instantly acceptable. Therefore, such concepts do not necessarily enhance a school's reputation.

We all know about the global marketplace and that in order to survive you must be competitive. You must be able to compete with the Japanese, the Germans, and the Taiwanese. If you cannot compete, you do not survive. So what is wrong with competition?

The paradox is that you cannot truly be competitive if you seek to be competitive.

The key word here is "survive." It is, of course, perfectly true that you must be competitive in order to survive. Giant retailers like Sears have to cut their costs considerably to be able to survive against other retailers such as Wal-Mart with its advanced computer systems and high sales per square foot. If your costs and values are out of line, you may cease to survive.

But any organization that plans just to survive will sooner or later find itself out of business. Only those organizations that plan for success will survive, while those that plan only to survive will fail.

So competition is important as part of the "baseline" for survival.

Picture an exotic garden outside Manila in the Philippines. A scented summer evening provides the perfect setting for a gourmet banquet for the Chevalier de Tastevins. Flaming torches are set among the bushes. Costumed waiters carry in the first dish of shellfish on their heads. Then follows clear soup in large earthenware bowls. Everyone, myself included, starts to spoon up the soup. It is very clear soup indeed. In fact it is not soup at all. It is plain water served in rather large finger bowls for rinsing the fingers after the shellfish dish. The mistake is understandable.

Water is necessary for soup—but soup has to be more than water.

In the same way there are many things that are necessary, but not sufficient, for business to survive (for example, cost control), just like water for the soup. Competition is one of the things that is necessary for business to survive, but it is not sufficient. A serious mistake that many executives make is to believe that competition is the key to success. It is not. Competition is merely part of the baseline of survival. Success requires going beyond competition to sur/petition.

Sur/petition

There is a serious overcapacity of about 25 percent in European car production. At one time I was giving a seminar for the British marketing department of Ford, the biggest Ford operation outside of Detroit. We were discussing competing in the European market.

I suggested that Ford should buy up a company called NCP (National Car Parks), which owned most of the car parks in city centers throughout the United Kingdom. If NCP became a Ford company, a notice could be placed at the entrance to all city center car parks indicating that only Ford cars could use them.

A car, I argued, is no longer just a lump of engineering. If your neighbor boasts that his lump of engineering is better than your lump of engineering, you can point out that you can park in the city, and he cannot. The ability to park is very much part of the "integrated value" of a car if you have to drive in a city. So is the ability to resell the car, have it serviced, and have it insured.

I have been told, for instance, that it is impossible to insure a Mercedes or a BMW if you live in the Bronx in New York.

It does not matter how good the engineering may be; if you cannot insure a car, you will probably not buy it.

Of course, Ford did not take up my idea. They said that as an engineering company, it was not their business to buy up car parks. In the future, some entrepreneurs probably will buy up or build car parks and then get the Koreans to make private-label cars for them. They will sell, park, insure, and resell cars. Manufacturing will only be a service to this profit center, and the manufacturing margins will be squeezed.

In the United States, car sales have been in decline for some time. There has been a five-year slide from sales of 16.3 million in 1986 to about 13.5 million in 1991. As everyone knows, the classic competitive response has been to slash prices and offer cash rebates. Surprisingly, competitors do the same. You may succeed in shifting sales forward in time, but then buyers get used to the rebates and wait for them before buying again.

The suggestion that Ford should have bought up the city-center car parks is an example of what I call sur/petition.

The word "com-petition" comes from the Latin and means "seeking together." It means "choosing to run in the same race." We could spell it as "(com)petition" to illustrate that all competitors are in the same race. The word "sur/petition" means "seeking above." Instead of choosing to run in the same race, competitors choose their own race. The slash in the new word "sur/petition" is there to indicate the notion of seeking "above," just as $\frac{2}{3}$ indicates two over three.

In addition, sur/petition is about creating "value monopolies." Some ways of achieving a monopoly are illegal, but value monopolies are not. For survival, you need competition, but for success you need sur/petition and the creation of value monopolies.

The difference between competition and sur/petition is illustrated in Figure I.1. Instead of running in the same race, you create your own race. Instead of seeking "together," you set out to seek "above."

Integrated Values

How do you create value monopolies? That is exactly what I shall be discussing in the body of this book. Value monopolies are driven by concepts, and concepts are in turn driven by serious creativity.

In order to understand value monopolies, you must realize that there have been three phases of business.

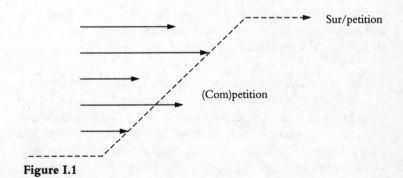

Sur/petition

(Com)petition

Figure I.1

The first phase was simply based on making available a product or service. It was production driven.

The second phase was based on competition, because a lot of people were now providing the same goods and services.

The third phase, which we are now just entering, is based on integrated values. No longer do we live in a world of simple values where a car is just a piece of engineering.

A good example of integrated values comes from Ron Barbaro, at one time head of the Prudential Insurance Company in Canada. Using some of my techniques of lateral thinking (serious creativity), he came up with the idea of "living benefits." This is a significant change in the very traditional business of life insurance, which has been unchanged for 120 years. With traditional life insurance, the benefits are paid out after your death to your family or other beneficiaries. Ron Barbaro's concept was to have 75 percent of the benefits paid out immediately if a policy holder was diagnosed as having a potentially fatal illness (such as cancer or AIDS). This meant that the money was now available for extra care or medical attention. The concept was immensely successful and was one of the reasons Ron Barbaro was soon promoted to head of Prudential in the United States.

This is an excellent example of integrated values because it integrates life insurance into the lives and values of people. There are single people, people who divorce and split up, children who grow up and become self-supporting, and many others. For some of them, many of the original purposes of life insurance are gone. At the same time there are factors like AIDS and the expense of medical care that create new purposes.

Barbaro created a simple concept change. Life insurance is traditionally seen as related to death; his concept emphasized life, and he had the courage and drive to see the concept through.

Concepts and Creativity

I have worked in forty-five countries, and I have found that the business community least happy with concepts is in the United States. There is an impatience with concepts and an urgent desire to be given "hands-on" tools. Americans want to be doing rather than thinking.

This is not surprising. For a long time the United States was a pioneer society, and in such a society action is indeed more rewarding than thinking: you need to clear a few more acres for grazing, drill a few more wells, open a few more stores. The great energy and lack of inhibitions in America also favor action.

Today, however, the world is more crowded. Unthinking action is not going to be rewarded. On the other hand, a concept change may be rewarded very handsomely. A new concept is unquestionably the best and cheapest way of getting added value out of existing resources.

Up to now, however, our approach to concept development has been very haphazard. There has been the "me-too" approach in which we wait for someone else to develop the concept, and then we jump in with a similar copy of it. In addition, we have assumed that as intelligent, able people we will come up with the needed concepts when necessary. This attitude to concepts is not good enough today.

In the future we are going to have to take concepts so seriously that we shall be setting up specific "Concept Research and Development" departments for the intellectual engineering that needs to take place. General Motors is said to spend about $5 billion a year on technical research and development, and Du Pont spends about $1.2 billion. Today, however, concepts are even more important than technology, and we shall have to take their development very seriously indeed.

Business schools have always taught students about how to analyze information and how to make decisions. Today this is totally inadequate. The analysis of information and decision making are part of the maintenance aspect of management, part of the water in the soup. The emphasis must now shift to conceptual thinking, not instead of information analysis and decision making, but in addition to them. What concepts are going to be derived from information analysis? By itself the analysis of information can never yield the concepts that are hidden in the information. What alternatives are available for decision making? Analysis can only yield some of the alternatives; the rest must be produced by creative design.

Unfortunately, the approach to creativity in the United States has been very weak. There is the mistaken notion that we are all basically creative, and it is only necessary to remove our inhibitions and fears of being ridiculous in order to release that innate creativity. That is why American creative methods have been crazy and off-the-wall.

We now know from the behavior of self-organizing information systems (like human perception) what we need to do. We know that the brain is not designed to be creative and that in order to be creative we have to use some methods that are "not natural." We must begin to develop systematic methods of serious creativity. I shall be discussing these later in the book, particularly their relevance to concept development.

In order to focus on serious creativity, I have set up an International Creative Forum to bring together those people in major corporations who are directly concerned with the development and application of creativity. Founding members of the Forum include IBM, Prudential, Du Pont, Merck, Nestle, British Airways (the world's largest international carrier), and BAA (the world's leading airport authority). I am happy to see that some major corporations are now beginning to take creativity seriously.

Valufacture

Concepts are about value. Sur/petition is also about value. The future success of any business is going to be all about value.

It has always seemed strange to me that although we deal so much with values, we do not have a specific word to describe the creation and formation of values. There is convenience in having such a word because it allows us to look at things in a different way and to devote much more effort to the specific creation of values. The new word that I propose in this book is "valufacture," which I define as "the creation and formation of values." There is an analogy with "manufacture," which has to do with the creation and production of objects.

The Age of Contraction

Many people in business feel that we have entered the age of contraction. There have been two ages of expansion. The first age of expansion was driven by marketing. Marketing was going to create needs and open up markets. Marketing was the main competitive tool for taking market share from others. The second age of expansion was driven by "gobble growth." You gobbled up other organizations in order to increase market share. During this period there were all sorts of rationalizations about market synergies and critical survival size (often provided by investment bankers who liked the fat fees involved).

The two ages of expansion have now passed. The present mood is for consolidation. Acquisitions have to be digested. Corporate executives are looking inward. There is cost cutting and slimming. There is a laying off of people. In five years CMS Energy Corporation trimmed its work force from 13,000 to 9,500. DEC (formerly Digital Equipment) wants to cut its payroll of 124,000 by 6 percent. There is divestment of unprofitable businesses everywhere.

As part of this looking-inward, there is an emphasis on cost cutting and cost control. There is an emphasis on quality management.

All these things are important and necessary, but they are not enough. You take aspirin when you have a headache, but you cannot survive on a steady diet of aspirin.

Figure I.2 shows that if you fall below the baseline of competence, you need to get back to that baseline. But just being on the baseline is not enough. You have to do better than that.

The purpose of consolidation, contraction, quality, and all the rest is to provide a firm baseline for venture. In the end you have to provide values that customers want. Having the best quality product at the lowest price is no good if that product does not offer significant value.

There is a serious danger that the current emphasis on what I would call "housekeeping" may divert attention from the very essence of a business, which is to provide saleable value. The essence of a business can be summed up in the following four "C" words:

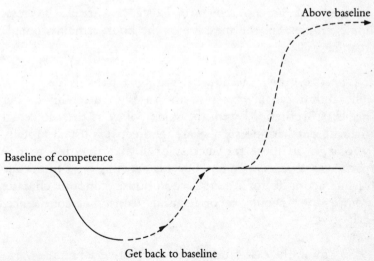

Figure I.2

- Competence: the quality, efficiency, effectiveness, and accomplishment of what you are supposed to be doing.

- Control: the cost control, strategy, and knowledge of what is going on.

- Care: care for the customer, for the work force, which is ultimately your most precious resource, and for the community (for example, environmental concerns).

- Creativity: the soul of the business. Without creativity you have a body with no soul. Creativity provides the value that is the whole purpose of any business.

Format of This Book

Everyone remembers the powerful effect of the book *In Search of Excellence* (Peters and Waterman). Most people know that many of the excellent corporations put forward in the book are no longer in existence—People Express, for example. Yet the message of the book remains: people matter.

The case-study method of writing a book is deceptive. The author can always pick the cases to meet his or her needs. Corporations with the same policy as the subject of the case but with no success are ignored. It is usually totally wrong to attribute the success of any corporation to one particular aspect of policy. Success depends on a multitude of interacting factors: market conditions, economic climate, competitors, people, labor relations, consumer confidence, and so on.

So I think the case-study method is not very honest. More importantly, it does not teach much beyond some general messages (valuable as these may be). It is far more important to lay out the message directly and to rely on the intelligence of the reader to relate the message to his or her own business circumstance.

This book is broadly divided into three parts.

Part I

- A look at some of the most fundamental habits of management thinking—efficiency, problem-solving, maintenance, and error-avoidance—and why even these fundamental habits need rethinking. While they may have been valuable in the past, they may now be inadequate and even dangerous.

- A look at the recent trends in management behavior: cost cutting, divestment, quality, customer service, gobble growth, and so on. While some of these trends are excellent, there are also negative aspects. For example, quality does not sufficiently consider quality of what and for whom.

Part II

- Sur/petition: the difference between traditional competition and sur/petition. The three phases of business and the nature of "integrated values," and the whole area of values in general.

Part III
- The practical "how to" section. Discussion of valufacture, the design of concepts, and concept research and development. The nature of serious creativity.

A New Perspective

One of the great advantages I have as an observer of business thinking is that while I work a great deal in the United States and Canada, I also spend a lot of time all over the world: Europe, Japan, Korea, South America—even the USSR and China. Often it is necessary to stand outside American business thinking in order to see clearly what is going on elsewhere. Certain habits are so traditional that from within the United States they are not even seen as peculiar. A global perspective is needed.

There is also a need to look across a wide range of businesses. Anyone running one particular business—no matter how successfully—simply cannot get this breadth of access. I have worked with electronics, computers, pharmaceuticals, food processors, beverages, chemicals, airlines, banks, and much more.

It has been my experience that the business sector has been the one sector of society to show most interest in "thinking" as such. Most other sectors of society like politics, and even the academic world, are more concerned with argument, proving that one side is right and the other is wrong. Government needs thinking very badly, but does surprisingly little of it. In business there is a reality test in the form of a bottom line. You can argue until you are blue in the face that you are right—but you can still go bankrupt.

Business handles the analytical side of thinking quite well. But there is a need for improvement in the constructive, creative, and conceptual side. In the future, this is the aspect of thinking that is going to be essential for success. All the rest is housekeeping. To be sure, you have to get the house-keeping right, and brilliant concepts are no substitute for good housekeeping. But housekeeping is not enough. Water is necessary for soup, but soup is more than water.

There is really only one serious disease in business thinking. This is the disease of arrogance and complacency, the feeling that "We are fine, we are doing well, we know it all." Fortunately for the rest of the world, the Japanese are beginning to catch this disease.

Summary

The new concepts to be introduced in this book are as follows:

1. Sur/petition, which goes beyond competition
2. "Integrated values" and the third phase of business
3. Valufacture and a new value notation
4. Concept R&D
5. "Serious creativity"

Edward de Bono

1

What Is Wrong with the Fundamentals?

Is there anything wrong with the fundamentals of business thinking such as efficiency, problem solving, analysis of information, and competition?

These fundamentals were developed in the early and somewhat primitive days of business, and though they are still valid today, there is a need to examine them more critically—which is what I intend to do in this section.

In the early days of business, the economic baseline was rising in developed countries and to a lesser extent in developing countries. It was only necessary to keep your place on this rising baseline and all would be well. The two things necessary to keep your place were efficiency and problem-solving.

Efficiency in the use of capital, people, energy, and resources could keep you on the rising baseline. If a problem arose, then you solved it and returned to the baseline. This process is shown in Figure 1.1.

The process is not unlike that of a family bringing up a child. There is shelter, care, and nutrition. If the child falls ill you call in the problem-solver, the doctor. The child is cured and goes on to grow into a healthy adult. Growth is the natural state of affairs.

Today, for a variety of reasons the baseline is flat and may even be declining. There is a global marketplace with over-production of goods and services — at least with regard to those who can pay for them. All the efficiency and problem solving in the world may only keep you "efficiently" on the declining baseline.

In short, efficiency and problem solving are maintenance procedures. If the direction is good or if the economic base-line is rising, then maintenance is sufficient; but if the baseline is not rising and the direction is not correct, then maintenance alone can never be enough.

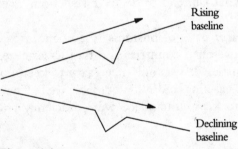

Rising
baseline

Declining
baseline

Figure 1.1

Businesses often feel that since they have a lot of market muscle and such a dominant position, maintenance will be enough. In recent years, however, even mighty IBM found that market domination was not enough if you fell behind on concepts. IBM fell behind on the concept of "connectivity" and has suffered as a result. IBM has also suffered from lower-priced clones when the mystique of computers wore off and there was no longer a need for reassurance from the solidity of Big Blue.

You may feel, therefore, that you have a secure market niche and that maintenance is enough. You may be correct in this assumption or you may not.

The maintenance concept of management used to be sufficient, but in most cases is not sufficient today.

I shall now have a look at each of the four fundamental pillars of traditional management thinking: efficiency, problem solving, information analysis, and competition.

Efficiency

Efficiency is the ratio between input and output. It asks, what is the best output that I can get for the resources that I put in? For this required output, what is the minimum of resources that I must put in? If we think in terms of efficiency, we have to think in terms of input/output ratios.

Efficiency means productivity. Efficiency means no waste. Efficiency means getting the best out of our efforts, energy, and resources. What can possibly be wrong about that?

To begin with, efficiency looks at input and output and does not look at the customer. The American auto industry removed all extras in order to give the customer the lowest-priced car. This is a form of efficiency. The Japanese built up their 30 percent of the American car market by piling on extras as part of the basic car price. This was not the working of the efficiency concept, but the working of another concept—effectiveness.

The Japanese are indeed very efficient, and such concepts as "just in time" are a witness to this efficiency. But they reach efficiency in a different way than American businesses. They reach efficiency through the route of effectiveness. The main difference is that efficiency is a ratio and effectiveness is not.

"Effectiveness" means that you determine exactly what you want to do. Then you use all the resources necessary to do it effectively. If you do not have enough resources to do everything, then you make a list of the things you want to do and go down that list using full resources for each item. When you have used up all your available resources, you stop.

Contrast this with efficiency, in which you divide all available resources among all the things you want to do.

If effectiveness means having five people paint one lamp-post, then you have five people paint the lamp-post. Efficiency means having five people paint five lamp-posts, even though the paint job might not be very good.

So the first stage in effectiveness is fulfilling the objective fully—whatever the cost in resources. The second stage is to turn to the effectiveness of the process itself. How can the process be made more effective? It is at this point that the process is improved and further improved. That is why there are far fewer parts in a Toyota than in a car from General Motors. The fewer parts make the assembly process more effective.

The end result of the whole process may seem to Western eyes to be efficiency, but it has been achieved by the double application of effectiveness, first to the output and then to the production process itself.

The principal efficiency question is, what are the minimum resources that I can use to get this output?

The effectiveness question is, how can the process be made more effective?

Effectiveness is not a ratio. The end point is fixed, and it is a matter of steadily improving the process of getting there.

There are further problems with the concept of efficiency. Efficiency is measurable at one point in time. While efficiency has to be measurable, what may happen in the future cannot be measured. So it is left out of any efficiency equation. You design a suspension system for the bumps it encounters right now, not for all the possible bumps it might encounter in the future. Efficiency has always got to look backward and historically. It seeks to maximize what is now being done and what is now known.

When the future turns out not to be exactly as predicted, which is usually the case, efficiency may actually have gotten us into trouble. Very efficient businesses are often very brittle. There is no cushion and no give, because there has been no waste and no slack. Bamboo scaffolding around major buildings in Hong Kong seems flimsy and insubstantial. In fact, it is very strong because it is flexible, and stresses and strains are shared all around.

Efficiency is often the enemy of flexibility, and in today's business world, flexibility is becoming more and more important. Flexibility, in fact, has been the key to the extraordinary economic development of the Asian Tigers (Hong Kong, Taiwan, Singapore, and Korea).

Instead of working towards being the most efficient bicycle producer in the world, a business must instead have a bicycle-making capacity. But if there is a downturn in bicycles, then that same business must switch part of its production to health equipment or prams or whatever is in demand. In the old days, designers of electrical generating stations used to wrack their brains to foresee the future cost of coal, oil, or gas so that their design would be the right one. Today they have given up such nonsense, and all power generators have a multifuel flexibility in order to use whatever fuel happens to be cheapest at the moment.

Too often, when we work toward efficiency, we forget about flexibility.

Problem Solving

It is easy to pick out the most dangerous saying in American business, a saying that almost by itself has been responsible for the decline in United States basic industry. Recovery has only come about by escaping from the saying, "If it isn't broken, don't fix it."

It's surprising that such a simple, and apparently sensible, saying could cause so much damage. It was meant to indicate that business should focus its thinking on problems and not worry about other matters—and that was precisely its danger.

Businesses were busy attacking and fixing their problems, and when they had fixed them, they were back to where they were before. Meanwhile their competitors were making changes at points that were not problems. They were busy changing the process itself, not just fixing problems in the existing process. For example, switching to continuous casting in the steel-making process boosted efficiency by 30 percent. And many of the mini-mill steel processes were pioneered in Italy and Mexico.

The danger of thinking only about problems is illustrated in Figure 1.2.

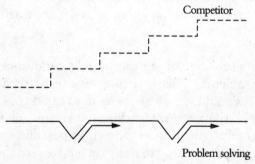

Figure 1.2

The chief executive of the General Electric company in England once told me that he was very happy when there were no problems in any of his many divisions. It is not surprising that that company had been sitting on a cash hoard of about $2.4 billion year after year without any attempt to use it for growth or development. Of course, they have not made the blunders that some others have made, but neither did they grow. The chief executive had done an excellent job in welding a group of motley and unsuccessful companies into one solid and profitable company. This was problem solving of the highest order. But these skills of problem solving were not applied to constructive growth.

At my seminars, if I ask a roomful of senior executives to put down a list of their corporate problems, they have no difficulty at all in putting down five, ten, or as many as I request. A problem is like a headache or a stone in your shoe. You know it is there, and you do not have to go out to look for it. But if I ask the same roomful of executives to put down points that are not problems but which might benefit from creative thinking, the result is totally different. Most of them have a hard time putting down even three points, and these are usually very vague and unfocused. Why is this so?

Almost all executives are thoroughly conditioned to look only at problems. This is a huge waste of their thinking capacity. I would even go so far as to say that most progress comes from thinking about things that are not problems. This is actually much easier since it is possible that no one else has thought about these things at all, so even the simplest ideas are still available.

We really need to think at three points. We do indeed need to think about problems, and that can be given priority provided it does not absorb all our thinking time and energy. But somehow we need to find time to think about things that are not problems—with a view to changing them or making them better. Finally, we should also find time to think about things that are going well. Why should we think about things that are going well? Why risk rocking the boat? Things may be going well through a match of market conditions and what we are doing. Rethinking the matter may provide even more benefit from those favorable market conditions. Under no circumstances should success be a barrier against further thinking. This is a far cry from thinking only about what is "broken."

Unfortunately, American psychology has gotten into the habit of using the term "problem solving" for all purposeful thinking. This is a very dangerous habit because it leads people to think only about problems while ignoring the creative and constructive opportunity thinking that should not be called "problem solving." This is an excellent example of how the wrong terminology can have unfortunate consequences.

This obsession with problem solving is especially Western and arises from the very core of Western thinking culture. This thinking culture was established during the Renaissance with the rediscovery of classical Greek thought (mainly through Arabic translations). Classical Greek thinking was a breath of fresh air after the emphasis on dogma that took place in the Dark Ages, so this new thinking was eagerly embraced both by the Church (which relished a "logical way" of proving heretics to be wrong)

and by the secular humanists, thinkers who wanted a thinking way to solve man's problems. It is hardly surprising
that this new mode of thinking took over Western society
through universities, seminaries, courts, and abbeys, and has
continued to dominate our thinking to this day.

This classic Greek thought was based on the gang of three.
There was Socrates, who was trained as a sophist and relished argument for the sake of argument. There was Plato,
who was somewhat anti-democratic (because the Athenian
democracy was running an incompetent war with Sparta),
and set up the notion of absolute ideas and truth. Then there
was Aristotle (pupil of Plato and tutor of Alexander the
Great), who established the principles by which objects and
ideas could be categorized. From this comes the principle of
contradictions and the basis of verbal Aristotelian logic. The
whole purpose of this thinking was to point out error and to
find fault. If we could remove these errors, it was assumed,
then we had the truth. So finding and pointing out error
has been the basis of Western thinking ever since. Hence our
obsession with problem solving.

The Western notion of improvement is to point out faults,
defects, and weaknesses, and then set about putting them
right. If we remove all faults, we believe, then the job has
been done. Contrast this with the Japanese culture, which
never had a Greek influence. They do not understand argument, but prefer parallel thinking. When it comes to improvement, they are also concerned with removing obvious
faults. But that is only the beginning, not the end, of the matter. The Japanese then go on to say, "this is perfect—so now
let us make it better." This is perhaps the single most significant difference between Western industrial thinking and
Japanese industrial thinking. The result is the Japanese habit

of continuous improvement, of improving things even when there are no faults at all. Today the West is busily trying to capture this habit with the current fashion for total quality management, about which I shall have more to say in another section.

Problem solving is usually urgent and has to take priority over other sorts of thinking. It is possible, however, to fill your life with so many urgent matters that there is no time left to think about truly important matters. Problem solving is attractive because the end and the benefits are obvious, and there is something tangible to work upon. Many executives feel happiest in a crisis, because survival is in itself achievement. Other types of thinking, such as opportunity development, are more speculative and more risky.

When we do have problems to solve, we are reasonably effective up to a point. The traditional technique is to analyze the problem, identify the cause of it, and then remove the cause. This is fairly straightforward from a thinking point of view. If you feel sharp pain when you sit down and identify that it is caused by a pin on your chair, then the cause can be removed and the problem solved. If you have a sore throat and identify the streptococcus bacilli involved, then an antibiotic will kill the bacteria and solve the problem. But there remains a whole class of problems for which this traditional approach does not work. There are problems where it is impossible to find the cause. There are problems with so many different causes that it is impossible to remove them all. There are problems where the cause is very obvious, but cannot be removed—perhaps because it is due to human nature itself. The current drug problem is a classic example. We can easily identify the causes, but do not seem able to remove them.

With problems where the cause cannot be removed, a different sort of thinking is needed. We need to be able to "design" a way forward. The emphasis is now on design rather than analysis. For design we need creativity and the ability to generate new concepts. None of our traditional thinking training provides such skills.

Information Analysis

The third fundamental of traditional business thinking is to collect information and then make decisions by analyzing and reacting to that information.

There was a time when executives were very short of information. Any improvement in information, therefore, would immediately improve the quality of the decisions that had to be made. In a sense, the information itself made the decisions. Today, however, we have computers that give us much more information and the ability to handle it. If a decision only requires more information, then that decision can be made directly by the computer without the need for human intervention.

The relationship between information and decision–value is suggested in Figure 1.3. At first, increasing information leads to better decisions, but after a while more and more information has less and less effect. There even comes a time when further information makes it difficult to sort out important information from the rest. There is confusion and information overload. Yet, as most data processing (DP) departments will confirm, executives faced with difficult decisions simply ask for more and more information in the hope

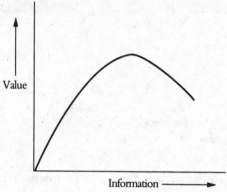

Figure 1.3

that somehow the new information will do their thinking for them.

In the past, information was indeed the bottleneck. Actions, decisions, and investments were held up for lack of information or had to be merely speculative. When dealing with the future, this is still the case today. On the whole, however, information is no longer the bottleneck that it once was. The information bottleneck has been opened up by computers and telecommunications.

A narrow bridge leads into a town. Traffic piles up before the bridge. A new, wider bridge is constructed. There is no longer the bridge bottleneck, so traffic flows on and piles up at the next bottleneck in town. The same thing happens with information. Information used to be the bottleneck. That bottleneck has been opened up (see Figure 1.4), but traffic now piles up before the next bottleneck. This next bottleneck is quite simply "thinking." Now that we have the information, what do we do with it?

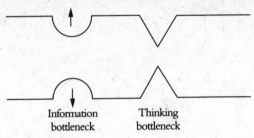

Information   Thinking
bottleneck   bottleneck

Figure 1.4

You have information that your competitor is offering financial rebates on cars. What do you do? You could follow the simple knee-jerk reaction of offering rebates yourself. The quality of your decision is not determined by the quality of the information you are getting, but by the quality of your thinking and the range of concepts you come up with.

In short, getting and using information is as important as it ever was, perhaps even more important, but it is not enough. In a more complex world, the way we use information becomes even more important.

We used to think that the analysis of information would in itself produce ideas. Today we know that this is not so and that the analysis of information can only allow us to select from ideas which we already have (although they can indeed be useful). In order to generate new ideas, however, we have to be able to do some idea work in our minds before coming to the information.

I shall be considering the very important relationship between information and concepts in a later section. Information by itself does not make concepts.

Competition

The traditional view of competitors is that they are enemies. This can be a very limiting view. One day the different
Japanese food companies got together and decided that it did
not make sense for each of them to have a half-empty truck
making a delivery to a supermarket. They decided to share
their transportation to the supermarkets. As a result there
was an 80 percent saving in delivery costs.

The Japanese are extremely good at distinguishing areas
where competition is necessary from areas where it is waste-
ful. For instance, there is intense competition between the
auto companies in Japan—much fiercer than in the United
States. They blitz each other with model changes, price
shifts, and anything else they can think of. Yet at lunch,
in the automakers club, they sit down every day to discuss
mutual problems. When they leave the premises, they are
competitors.

It is true that in the United States, concerns about antitrust
laws make life much more difficult, and American industry
is put under a severe disadvantage—not by the laws themselves, which seek to prevent cartels and price fixing, but by
a too-wide interpretation of the law.

Basic research, for example, is an area in which competitors
can get together. Indeed there are already two consortiums in
the United States in which manufacturers of semiconductors
have come together to cooperate on basic research.

In the securities industry there is often overcapacity in data
processing, and this too could be shared with competitors.

So can back-office research, which may be too expensive for one organization.

But if you have an antique shop and someone sets up another antique shop near you, should you not be concerned about this competition? Not at all. The more antique shops, the more the area will be visited by antique buyers. Similarly one hotel does not make a resort, but several competing hotels will increase business for all of them by providing a critical mass for infrastructure development, travel agent consciousness, and other endeavors.

When Kodak ventured into the instant camera business a few years ago, analysts marked down Polaroid stock. But, in fact, Polaroid's sales increased because Kodak now had to advertise instant cameras.

So the traditional view of competitors as enemies may not always be correct. The key is to decide in which areas they are actually beneficial and in which areas they are rivals. It is not so much a win/lose situation but a win/win/lose situation.

Nevertheless, you do have to keep up with the competition or you will be out of business. Nothing could be more fundamental than that. The traditional tools have been price, quality, product differentiation, and market segmentation, and all these still have their value.

Although the airline industry may be sustaining heavy losses, the richer airlines still see a value in offering frequent-flyer schemes in the hope of knocking the less-secure airlines out of the skies. Classical competition still works.

The danger, however, is when our thinking is limited to this classic view of competition.

As I have indicated in the introduction to this book, competition at its basic level is necessary for survival, as is cost control and production efficiency. A business cannot afford to be left behind. But this is not enough. There is also a need to move forward, and this is where sur/petition comes in.

A few years ago, Du Pont developed a carpet fiber that would resist stains (Du Pont makes fibers but not carpets). This new fiber was offered to the carpet mills, but they were not very interested. Du Pont then launched an advertising campaign directed at the general public. Because the Stainmaster carpet was such an excellent example of integrated value, the demand from the public was such that the mills were forced to make the carpets, along with increased profits. Within three years Stainmaster carpets had something like 70 percent of the carpet market. Interior designers were recommending light-colored carpets, but such carpets were easily wrecked by stains. People living in smaller apartments did not have any special place for feeding youngsters, so carpet stains were likely to happen. Buying carpets became not just a matter of better colors, longer wear, or cheaper prices as in classic competition. The value of Stainmaster carpets clearly integrated into the lifestyle of the buyers. This is an excellent example of sur/petition.

The difference between competition and sur/petition will be considered in greater detail in the section specifically devoted to this comparison.

2

Recent Fashions in Business Thinking

Fashions in business thinking are determined by fashion, by cycles, by economic trends, and by social values. Fashion simply means that other people seem to be thinking the same way, so it becomes the accepted way to think. In the same way, cycles come and go. A cycle of expansion is often followed by a cycle of contraction. Worldwide and local economic trends also affect thinking. Businesses, for instance, tend to think differently during a recession. Finally, social values such as environmental consciousness change the playing field. All of these fashions are superimposed on fundamentals such as cost-cutting, restructuring, quality management, human resources, and environmental concerns.

Cost-Cutting

An emphasis on cost-cutting has been going on for more than a decade. It is currently driven by several factors:

1. It is necessary to cut unit costs in order to be competitive both on the home market, against imports, and even more so on the export market. The low dollar helps.

2. People are very expensive.

3. After the expansion days of the 1980s, there is a need to consolidate.

4. In times of recession, there is little prospect of market growth so the emphasis is on profitability through improving the bottom line by cost-cutting.

Cost-cutting is always attractive to management. On the whole, it is a low-risk area and the cost saved is more directly translated into increased profitability than is the revenue from new ventures. Cost-cutting is also attractive because it is something you can get your teeth into. Cost-cutting is attractive because everyone can get involved, unlike strategy-planning, which only takes place at senior levels.

General Motors has reduced costs by 15 percent since 1987, though it is still behind Toyota. Citicorp plans to lay off 8,000 people in 1991. The overexpanded securities industry is looking for a further reduction of 20,000 people after a similar reduction in 1990.

The cost of an average Hollywood film has soared to $30 million, so there is a search for ways to cut this rising cost. General Motors spends $622 of the cost of each car or truck on health benefits for its workers. About $400 of an automobile insurance premium is allocated to legal costs. Everywhere there is a search for ways of cutting costs. If the thickness of a steel slab in the production process is reduced from ten inches to two inches, the labor costs will be halved and energy reduced by about 30 percent.

Organizations do grow fat because of good times, drift, and loss of control, so cost-cutting at first yields big benefits. But the benefits get less and less as the easiest fat is removed. The competitive benefits of cost-cutting come through early if your main competitors are slow to cut their costs, but as soon as they start to keep pace the competitive advantage disappears (see Figure 2.1). So cost-cutting as a periodic exercise and cost-control as a permanent attitude are going to show good immediate results, but the benefits are not going to be continuous. The strategy is not sufficient.

The same danger applies to cost-cutting as applied to efficiency. There is the danger of forgetting the future and so paring costs that future development is at risk. There are activities which simply cannot be justified by a present judgment, but only by a potential future payoff. If such activities are dropped, the balance sheet looks better for the moment, but there is nothing to fuel the future. Projects are often postponed if they cannot immediately justify their costs. This permanent attitude of cost-consciousness can

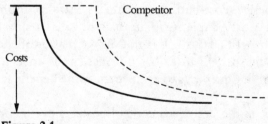

Figure 2.1

quite easily lead to dangerous penny-pinching. For example, there can be cutbacks in communication costs and training.

Tony O'Reilly of Heinz gives a good illustration of the dangers of cost-cutting. The number of workers in a tuna-processing plant were reduced. The result was that a lot of the tuna meat was left on the skeleton and thrown away. The company was forced to increase the number of workers, which again led to an increase in costs but also to a much greater increase in revenue from the additional tuna meat recovered. The moral is simple. Cutting costs by simply reducing the number of people involved may be counterproductive.

The Russian planning agency Gosplan had a very simple method. You took the production figures of any given business organization and added 10 percent. If this production goal was not achieved, then someone was to blame—and heads would roll. Many organizations act in a similar way. They ordain a 10 percent cut in the work force, and then let subordinates figure out how to get the work done with fewer people. It makes a lot more sense to restructure the work first, and then see how many people are now required.

In practice, cost-cutting requires a great deal more creativity than most people imagine. It is not just a simple matter of cost-benefit analysis. It is not only a matter of choosing to give up the benefit if it does not justify the cost. It is also a matter of finding ways to achieve the same benefit at less cost.

Which is the better, to control costs at every moment or to go through periodic cost-cutting exercises? The simple answer is to say both. I think the real answer depends on the nature of the business. If little venture is required, then permanent tight cost-control might be better in order to prevent cost-drift. But if the business does require venture, then periodic cost-cutting exercises may be better, for permanent cost-control could seriously inhibit new ventures.

Divestment is often a traditional part of cost-cutting. If 80 percent of your profit comes from 20 percent of your business, then why not get rid of the unprofitable 80 percent? Many organizations do exactly this, and it works—up to a point. Beyond that point you may be getting rid of growth and development areas. If you carry the 80/20 principle far enough, you will always find at every stage that some areas are producing relatively more profits than others. For instance, General Motors may find that it is getting more profits out of GMAC (its finance arm) than out of making cars. So should GM stop making cars? An organization that carries the 80/20 principle to extremes ends up as an investment company that is making nothing except investments.

Restructuring

Banks in the United States are said to have some $150 billion on their books as a result of the restructuring frenzy of the 1980s. Many people discovered what the Japanese call "zai-tek" or the technology of making money with money. The Japanese are learning to love this game, with the result that the Nikkei index will be much more volatile in the future than it has been in the past.

However, the restructuring game is mostly over. In 1990 mergers and acquisitions were down by a third, and investment banks have had to shed staff. The fat fee days seem to be over for the time being.

It makes more sense to buy up a market share rather than build it. Building it is competitive, expensive, and risky. Buying up another organization makes sense so long as the price is not inflated (which it usually is) and so long as the cash flow can cover interest payments. The advertising agency WPP came from nowhere to become the largest advertising agency in the world by buying J. Walter Thompson, Ogilvy and Mather, and other agencies. Now WPP is in trouble with the debts it incurred. Saatchi and Saatchi followed the same route with similar end results. To be a financial wizard, you need a rising market, a short memory, and a friendly bank. When the market stops rising, you could be in trouble.

It makes sense to buy up companies with successful innovations in technology, software, chemicals or other areas. In this way you are buying only success. Otherwise, you would have to invest in many failures in order to get the occasional success. Again the policy makes sense if the price is right.

Quite apart from the macho need to grow bigger, there is the sense that there is a critical size for survival in the global market. There are certain areas, like chip production, where the costs of development get ever higher, and only the really big boys can survive. Insurance companies have wanted to be financial supermarkets. In England, the Prudential company bought up real estate agents as a way of getting access to housing loans. That part of the business has now been sold at a great loss. Insurers have decided they do not want to be financial supermarkets any more and are now focusing on market niches and specialties.

The interesting thing about gobble-growth thinking is that you can construct a very rational argument for getting bigger and then an equally rational argument for getting smaller again. The stock market, for example, does this all the time. A corporation is marked up for making a judicious acquisition because people are sold the story of critical size, global markets, synergy, and diversification. Then when the organization is large enough, it suddenly becomes clear that it would have a higher value if it were broken up and sold off as separate bits. In most cases, economic realities are far less important than the up-and-down game which all investors have to encourage if they are going to make any living at all.

Gobble-growth has always seemed a short cut. In many cases it fails because synergies fail to develop, different corporate cultures cannot be combined, or too high a price was paid. There are even times when it still makes sense. But its main danger is that it swamps and excludes the sort of thinking that chief executives should be doing to develop their own organizations. The gobble-growth route is so much easier, so much more attractive, and often so much more personally rewarding (both in macho and financial terms).

Quality Management

"Total quality management" is very much in fashion. It is a successful attempt to capture the Japanese notion of improvement. As I indicated earlier, the Western notion of improvement has been restricted to removing faults, whereas the Japanese notion of improvement has been one of progressive improvement even when there have been no faults at all. Quality management seems a wonderful way of getting people more motivated and more interested in whatever they are doing. Like cost-cutting, quality management can be everyone's business. There can be programs, work discussion groups, quality circles, and other group involvement.

Organizations like Nordstrom and Limited Inc. have built considerable reputations in quality service.

Quality management usually includes, or at least overlaps, the other fashion of "customer first." Jan Carlzon of S.A.S. airlines achieved considerable fame with his reminder to the airline staff that in the end, the customer paid their salaries. The recognition of the importance of the customer was long overdue. The matter is not fully worked out even today. Many organizations with "customer-first" programs have not yet learned to distinguish between charm and service. Charm is being agreeable and polite to customers, and this is well worthwhile in itself. Service is what you do when things go wrong. On the whole, airlines have improved more on the charm side than on the service side.

There is a fatal flaw in the quality approach. This is finding the answer to two questions: quality of what? and quality for what? If you were making manual typewriters, you could greatly improve their quality, but this would not in itself prevent you going out of business when electronic typewriters took over. Gestetner, a manufacturer of duplicating equipment, had exactly this problem. The company thought that the development of electronics would be too expensive and that there would always be a niche for high-quality duplication. There was not, and in the end, they had to change.

Recent Fashions in Business Thinking

Quality may involve a company more intensely in whatever it is doing. The dilemma is that while this is necessary and beneficial, it may at the same time prevent change.

The usual answer to this dilemma is to say that quality is not directed at what is being done, but at the purpose of what is being done. So you do not make better manual typewriters; you make better typewriters—which may be electronic. But is this enough? What about computers and word processors, which are better ways of handling written material. The process is unending and so nebulous that, in practice, quality tends to be directed at what is being done at the moment. This concern for present quality does have a high value, provided that someone is questioning whether it is the right thing to do.

In all those things that have become obsolete, would a higher degree of quality have prevented that obsolescence?

People Care

Executives in the Western countries have come to realize that people are their most precious resources. Participation management, flattening hierarchies, motivation, and leadership are all part of this "people religion."

The Japanese handle things in a totally different way. First of all, in Japan there is much less job mobility and so less impatience with things. This is changing as the Japanese learn the worst Western habits and the West picks up the best Japanese habits. The hierarchical rigidity of a Japanese organization, and the immense respect for age and authority, actually permit a greater flow of ideas. This is because senior people are secure and are not threatened by junior employees with bright ideas. The senior person knows that he is not there because he has the best ideas. He is there to listen to the ideas of others. In addition, the Japanese divide their workday into two rigid sections. In the first part, they do as much as they are told to do. At the end of the work day, they all go off to drink together—and that is where participative management takes place. There is now informality, discussion, and exchange of ideas. The result is that husbands do not usually get home until late into the night. In fact, wives get so used to being without husbands that when the husbands eventually retire, their wives are apt to divorce them because the husbands are now nuisances and in the way.

Human Resource and training officers used to be fairly lowly creatures in American organizations. Suddenly they find themselves of much greater importance. People now matter. Nevertheless, the commitment to training is nowhere near as serious as in Japanese companies. Whenever a Japanese company sets up in a Western country with Western workers, the most striking thing that is noticed is the intensive and rigorous training that Japanese training officers give the workers. With the training goes a much higher degree of responsibility. A Japanese worker has the right to stop the production line.

There is the old definition of a camel as being a horse designed by a committee. Democracy is not the most efficient way of designing things or of getting things done. The trick in participative management is to get involvement and motivation, and yet constructive movement forward. Obviously, that is where leadership comes in. The greater the participation, the greater the need for superior leadership.

There is a conventional Western belief that creativity is best done in groups as a "brainstorming" session. In my experience this is probably a fallacy. Creative individuals working on their own seem to produce a wider range of ideas than when they are working as a group. The reason is that as a group, there has to be a lot of listening, and thus the directions taken are far fewer. One of the original purposes of the group format was to provide a stimulus from outside one's own thinking in order to allow the mind to take a different direction. This is no longer necessary because with the deliberate techniques of lateral thinking that I shall be describing later in the book, individual thinkers can now provide their own outside stimulation. There is still merit, however, in having ideas discussed, at the second stage, in a group because others may be able to take an idea further than can the originator of that idea.

There is the additional danger when everything is done in groups that the more socially dynamic people will exert an undue influence and the more retiring people will tend to get ignored. Since there is not an automatic correlation between social dynamism and business effectiveness, this may not be a good thing.

Environmental Concerns

The furrier industry is going out of business. McDonald's has dropped the polystyrene containers that used to keep hamburgers warm. Recycled paper proudly proclaims itself.

By 1995 there must be a cleanup of gasoline in nine major U.S. cities, and the equipment for this could cost $25 billion. The modified Clean Air Act might cost utilities as much as $105 billion by the year 2010. Smoking is banned on many flights and in many workplaces.

All of these concerns about the environment are more than a fashion. Very often it is schoolchildren who first learn environmental values from their teachers and then act as missionaries by taking these values home. When these children grow up, they will be even more environmentally conscious than their parents.

Environmental concerns, however, provide problems, costs, opportunities, and a considerable amount of public-relations effort. There are successful venture funds that invest only in environmentally safe corporations. There are manufacturers who hope to gain market share by labeling their products as environmentally friendly.

On the other hand, environmental values provide whole new directions for research. Chemical companies seek to provide biodegradable products. Plastic bags are now being made from starch derivatives.

Any major shift in values calls for new thinking. There are, of course, those who hope these values are just a fashion and that the pressures will abate. There are others who see an opportunity and jump on the bandwagon. As with any fashion, the best thing to do is to be slightly ahead of the game. Being too far ahead is expensive and unrewarding. Being too far behind means that the costs are the same, but the benefits are fewer.

Concern for environmental values is being closely followed by quality-of-life values. People will be concerned with where they work, how long they work, under what conditions they work, and how much time they have for their families, and so on. Consumers will tend to buy more durable goods and hold on to their cars longer.

The distinction between being "busy" and "working" will become more obvious. Flexible working hours and working out of the home will separate real work from merely being busy and filling the usual workday. Automation, computers, and telecommunications will make this more possible. A cartoonist I know works miles away from his newspaper and communicates by fax.

These newer values will initially be forced on to business, but will then be embraced by business as part of conventional business thinking.

3

Complacency

Each time the French want to say the number 97 in the course of everyday shopping, they say: "quatre-vingt-dix-sept" (four times twenty and ten and seven). That seems an immensely cumbersome way of saying 97, but they have become used to it. It seems perfectly normal to them—or, one might say, they have become complacent. Complacency is when things seem normal to you because you are used to them.

Any business is really an "idea machine" as suggested in Figure 3.1. At one end of the machine are fed in the resources: capital, raw materials, management, labor, machinery, energy. The *idea machine* fashions these into a product or service according to the forming idea. What comes out at the other end is a product or service which can be sold at a good enough price to keep the machine running, to satisfy present investors, and even to entice future ones.

With the single exception of acquisitions, all the habits of management thinking that I have discussed are concerned

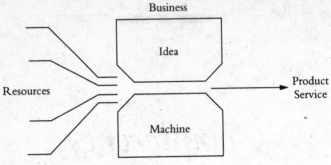

Figure 3.1

with keeping the machine running. They are concerned only with maintenance. They are concerned with providing the baseline. As I have suggested earlier, this kind of thinking was sufficient at one time, but it is not sufficient today. It is indeed necessary—but not sufficient. In no case have I challenged the validity of conventional thinking habits because each habit is still valid. There are some cautions that I have pointed out, but these do not detract from the basic validity of such trends as quality, people care, problem solving, and cost-cutting. What I do strongly challenge, however, is the sufficiency of these concepts. Being content with the adequacy of our current thinking habits is a dangerous complacency.

Perhaps the very word "management" is at fault. Imagine a stagecoach with a team of spirited horses. The driver has a hard time managing the team. The word "management" implies that the energy, the ideas, the resources, the people, and the markets are all there—and all that is needed is someone to manage these various things. Management is like driving a car along a difficult road. Skills or guidance are called for, and if the car breaks down you repair it to keep it going. But you are not choosing the car or the road.

Management is all about housekeeping. It is assumed that the existing core ideas are valid. Energy is applied to the idea machine in order to keep it running, not to the idea itself.

I once coined the expression Catch 24. This can be stated as follows: "in order to reach the senior position in an organization, you should be without, or have kept hidden, exactly those talents you will need when you get there." (This is parallel to the Peter Principle that holds that everyone is promoted to his or her level of incompetence, and is one catch more than Catch 23, which states that "something may be a very good idea–except at any particular point in time." *Catch 22,* of course, is the title of Joseph Heller's novel.) At lower levels, problem-solving and housekeeping skills are most important and are what get noticed. People are indeed promoted for these types of abilities. But at the most senior level there is a need for conceptual, creative, and strategic thinking. Mere problem solving can be delegated to others.

Housekeeping is very necessary, but there is also the venture aspect. That is also necessary. What are the values that you are selling? What are the core ideas of the idea machine? This is where sur/petition becomes so important because competition is really part of the housekeeping and baseline maintenance.

There was a time when strategic planning was much in vogue. People used to plan with great formality where a company should be in the future. Strategic planning fell into disfavor when the future refused to play the role assigned to it by the planners. The sheer unpredictability of the future, the rapid rate of change, the instability and positive feedback loops in nonlinear systems made a nonsense of planning. At best, there had to be a sort of rolling strategic plan with reassessments almost every week.

So the emphasis shifted away from strategic planning to another concept. This was the concept of being fit, lean, and muscular, and quick on your feet. In this way, your organization could respond effectively and profitably to any situation that arose. If an opportunity opened up, like the reunification of Germany or the opening of Eastern Europe, then you could move in right away. If market conditions changed, you could change with them. If technology offered new directions, you could be quick to jump in with a "me-too" product. When SKF launched the immensely successful Tagamet product for the treatment of peptic ulcer, Glaxo quickly jumped in with Zantac, which was even more successful. Almost 70 percent of the effort in certain chemical R&D departments is devoted to finding ways around other people's patents.

With this retreat from forward planning to corporate fitness and speed of response, the emphasis was back on housekeeping, because excellent housekeeping was what made an organization fit.

Take Germany, for example, a nation with a hugely successful economy. It is, in relative terms, the biggest exporting nation in the world. Yet when German executives were asked to rank creativity among other items needed for success, they put creativity lower on the list than any other developed nation. So here was a very successful industrial economy that put all the emphasis on quality and little on creativity. In time, this lack of attention to creativity will have its effect. Already Germany has fallen far behind in electronics and is trying to catch up through joint ventures with the Japanese.

How then does one account for the success of the German economy? That success is due to the excellence of the engineering quality. That, in turn, is due to an apprenticeship scheme that is unequalled anywhere else in the world, providing a highly skilled and motivated engineering work force.

If you produce quality cars, people will buy them. The Japanese are now muscling into this market and in some cases are outstripping the Germans, because the Japanese have both quality and innovation. If you produce high-quality machine tools and capital goods, then people want to buy them. No matter how high the cost may be, the quality is worth having. Indeed, if the cost is high enough, then the machine becomes a good discriminator; the successful business can afford such a machine, and the less successful one cannot and so gets left behind.

So quality does have to come first. The United States and other countries have tended to put innovation before quality. That does not work. Quality has to be the baseline—and that is why Germany has been so successful.

But when others can also provide quality, innovation comes into its own.

The Japanese are great innovators. They are not very good at individual creativity (though there are many exceptions, such as Honda himself) but they take the game of creativity seriously. They are, however, great innovators because they are willing to try out and put into production almost any idea they have. Within Japan, corporations blitz each other with streams of new products. Competitors immediately "cover" these products just in case they should turn out to be successful. Even while they are launching one product, a company often already has in an advanced stage of product development the next generation of products and the one after that. They believe very little in market research and analysis within their own country. They prefer to get the product out into the marketplace and use the actual test of the market. People will buy the product, they believe, or it will disappear. Something like 1000 new soft drinks are put out on the market every year, and almost every one of these fails and disappears. Once again we see the difference between efficiency (market analysis, testing, and so on) and effectiveness. It is perfectly true that the Japanese home-market loves gadgets and new things. These same companies do not adopt the same procedure abroad.

The main point is that while the Japanese are much concerned with the housekeeping side of things (they provided the inspiration for quality, 'just in time,' and so on) they are also concerned with the venture side of innovation. Western companies sometimes think it is enough just to get the housekeeping right. Everyone knows that Japanese quality owed its origins to the American Edward Deming, who was then largely ignored in the United States because the emphasis was on market development. Today the pendulum has swung too far the other way. There is an obsession with quality to the neglect of venture.

Types of Complacency

I want to discuss four types of complacency. These overlap a great deal but are still separable. The four types are comfortable complacency, cozy complacency, arrogant complacency, and lack-of-vision complacency.

Comfortable Complacency

" . . . we are doing all right."

" . . . we get by."

" . . . we have our own little niche."

" . . . we survive."

" . . . we just keep going day-to-day."

The Australian airline QANTAS (the oldest airline in the world) used to be very profitable and had a load factor of over 80 percent on its long-haul routes. Its strategy was very simple: provide fewer flights than the market needed. That way your planes would always be full. At that time, Australian air traffic was tightly regulated, and foreign airlines were not allowed to land in Australia (with very few exceptions). The situation today is different, and the airline's comfortable policy can no longer be used.

There are other examples of comfortable complacency. If you run a small family restaurant that provides a reasonable income for your family, why try to expand?

If you have a successful small business, you may not want to make your little niche too big, because the big boys might move in to the area.

Cozy Complacency

If there is a wild winter outside, you tend to snuggle down by the fire and make things as comfortable as you can inside the house.

Similarly, if there is a recession, you cut down on your ventures, batten down the hatches, and ride out the storm. If consumers are not buying because they have no confidence, no money, and no loans, then there is no point in venture-thinking. Focus instead on housekeeping. In time, things will change. Business runs in cycles, and boom times will return.

" . . . now is the time to get ourselves in shape."

" . . . we can postpone that project for the time being."

" . . . we cannot increase sales, so we must cut costs."

Arrogant Complacency

This is the complacency that comes from believing that you know it all, that you have all the answers. Today the Japanese are coming close to that sort of arrogance, and they may find it to be dangerous in the long run. Taizo Yakushiji feels that Japan has indeed become complacent and arrogant. He says that to be a true leader, Japan must be prepared to share its technology, just as much of Japan's success once depended on the rest of the world sharing its technology with Japan.

" . . . we are very successful, we must be doing it right."

" . . . we have nothing to learn, we do the teaching."

" . . . we are the world leaders in this field."

Confidence is an energizer, but complacency destroys energy. There is a very fine line between the two. I have found several American companies far too complacent about the efforts they are making in the field of creativity. This surely is a field in which no one can really afford to be complacent.

Lack-of-Vision Complacency

In one of my previous books I wrote about the "village Venus effect." If your horizons are limited to the small village in which you live, then the prettiest girl in the village becomes the ultimate Venus because you cannot imagine anyone more beautiful. If your horizons are limited and you lack any vision of what might be, then you have to be complacent.

This is the most common form of complacency, and it is very difficult to counter. That is why so many organizations seek out leaders with vision. If the leader has no vision, then the outlook for the organization is poor in the long run. It will survive from day-to-day and manage the crises that arise, but ultimately there is little prospect of success.

"... I cannot see what more can be done."

"... we are doing as well as anyone else."

"... convince me that we should be doing something else."

Evolution

There are many who believe that change should be brought about by evolution. You solve problems and survive crises.

Pressure of competition and the marketplace gradually mold what you should be doing. Business often sees this as safer than design, because design can often go drastically wrong.

Yet in system terms evolution is a most inefficient way of getting change. With evolution, each next step is determined by where you are at the moment. As long as a path is not actually disastrous, we follow along that evolutionary path. Yet this path may be far from making the optimal use of what is available.

Imagine a sequence of cardboard pieces that you are given one after the other, as in Figure 3.2. At each point, you have to make the best use of what you are given. The best use means moving as directly as possible from A in the direction of B. It is quite clear that the "best" positioning of the pieces at every step is far from the optimal use of them. Optimal use becomes possible, however, if we escape from the arrival sequence of the pieces to arrange all the pieces in the best possible way. This is why step-by-step evolution is so ineffective. It is also one of the reasons why there is an absolute need for creativity in thinking—otherwise we cannot escape from the time sequence of our experience.

Nominated Champions

Sir Colin Marshall, the chief executive of British Airways, the world's largest international carrier, tells how he eventually discovered that unless there was a "nominated cham-

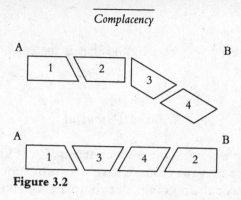

Figure 3.2

pion" who was given responsibility for making something happen, then nothing ever did happen. This has also been my experience with creativity within organizations. Creativity is a wonderful thing which finds favor with everyone, and most organizations claim to be creative— at least in their corporate advertising. Yet nothing much gets done beyond this lip service, because what is everyone's business becomes no one's business. This fact was realized by Du Pont, which appointed David Tanner as its "process champion" for creativity within the organization. As a consequence, Tanner has been responsible for building up the attitudes and skills of creativity in an impressive way.

The need for nominated champions indicates that complacency is not usually a conscious choice. It just happens. Things just settle down. As long as matters are proceeding smoothly, there is satisfaction—whether justified or not. But there is no easy way to tell, and that is the essential danger of complacency.

Unused Potential

Complacent organizations are not necessarily headed for disaster because they may indeed have a niche or enough market muscle to keep them going. But complacency almost always means unused potential. If you have a powerful and effective organization, there is a great deal that can be done. The energy and the channels are there. All that may be lacking is the direction. Yet many powerful organizations are so risk averse and individuals are so scared of making mistakes, that this huge potential is unused.

A research department might turn up ten new products, but the strategy and resources of the organization may only allow the top four to be used. Product number five, however, may be an excellent product that someone else might have been very happy to have developed. Because there are four other products that better fit the needs of the organization in no way means that the fifth one is unusable. In practice, nothing much usually happens with this fifth product or the ones after it. Occasionally, someone who has been involved in the development of the product is able to buy it out and set up a new venture. That, in fact, is how Gore-Tex began—with a product which Du Pont did not intend to develop.

There is a need here for what is called "cuckoo investment," in which outside investors provide the resources for the product to be developed within the framework of the organization on some agreed-upon buy-out basis. Either the organization can buy out the outside investors and take the developed product back in-house, or the outside investors can buy out the shares held by the major organization and take the product away on their own.

So the twin dangers of complacency are:

1. Slow drift and decline
2. Unused potential and opportunities

4

The Four Wheels of Human Thinking

A car has four wheels. Each of the four wheels is important. If it had only three wheels, you could point out the clear need for a fourth by showing the inadequacy of three. But this is not to attack any of the three existing wheels, each of which is essential. Each of the wheels is necessary, but not sufficient. As readers will have noticed, that phrase "necessary but not sufficient" is a recurrent theme in this book. Water is necessary for soup, but not sufficient.

In my experience the message of "necessary but not sufficient" is very hard to put across to people. We are much more used to the kind of direct attack in which we say that something is "wrong" and should be replaced by something which is "right." This is much more in our tradition of argument thinking in which we set out to prove that one point of view is right and the other is wrong.

Business thinking is human thinking in the end. It is true that, in many cases, our thinking has been concerned only with description, analysis, and argument, and that we have falsely elevated that sort of thinking to a high esteem. Business thinking has to be practical and constructive. Business thinking is concerned with making things happen. Business thinking has a reality test in the end: does the organization function, and will the market buy the product?

1. Procedures and Routines

Someone once used an IBM computer to work out the number of ways of getting dressed with eleven items of clothing. The computer was not allowed to learn from experience. The computer took 45 hours of non-stop computation. This is not really surprising, because with eleven items of clothing the number of possible combinations is given by multiplying $11 \times 10 \times 9 \times 8$ and so on. This gives over 39 million combinations. If we were to try one out every minute of our life, we would have to live to be eighty years old and use all our waking life trying out ways of getting dressed. Life would be rather difficult.

Of course, the human brain does not work like that. The brain works as a self-organizing system in which incoming information organizes itself into patterns and sequences.

There is a huge difference between "passive" or externally-organized information systems and self-organizing information systems. In passive systems, information is laid passively on a surface and has no activity of its own. An external organizer, or processor, uses that information and moves it around. All our traditional information systems are of this sort. In active systems the information and the surface are both active. The result is that the information organizes itself.

In a remarkably simple manner, the nerve networks in the brain operate as a self-organizing system that allows incoming information to organize itself into sequences. This is not unlike rain falling on a landscape and eventually organizing itself into streams and rivers (except that in the brain the landscape is not fixed). When I wrote about these things in 1969 (*The Mechanism of Mind*),* the ideas were quite strange at the time. Today they are fully accepted mainstream thinking. In fact, there are introductions by three Nobel prize-winning physicists to my latest book *I am right—you are wrong*,† in which I bring these ideas up-to-date, using them as a basis for challenging traditional Western thinking habits. We now know a great deal more about self-organizing systems and we are beginning to apply this knowledge to areas such as economics, where it should make a big difference.

So the brain is designed to make sense of the world around us by forming routine patterns of perception from incoming information. That is how we learn. That is also how we live, how we get by. The brain is designed to be routine. The brain is not designed to be creative, and we should be immensely grateful for its wonderful design. Without it life would be a confused impossibility. So the brain gets us to see things in the usual and traditional way. All we need to do is to trigger a routine pattern, and then that is what we see. The mind

---

*Simon & Schuster, New York, 1989; Jonathan Cade, London, 1989; Penguin, London, 1977.

†Viking/Penguin, London, 1990; Viking, New York, 1991.

can only see what it is ready to see. That is why the analysis of data cannot yield new ideas.

Organizations behave rather like the brain. Informal patterns of communication and behavior are set up and used. In an organization there are also the formal patterns, procedures and routines which are set up deliberately and by design. Just as in the brain, the purpose of these patterns is to tell us what to do on any particular occasion so that we do not have to work things out each time. While to some extent these routine procedures are restricting, on the whole they are immensely useful.

The purpose of intense Japanese on-the-job training, for example, is to make sure these routine patterns are available when required. The purpose of military drill and training is similarly to get coordinated action.

Ideally, a business should have all its routine patterns available, plus the flexibility to decide which pattern to use.

In any production process, we set up systematic procedures. We can refine, improve, and change these procedures, but there do have to be procedures in the first place. The more rigid the procedures, the more possible it becomes to use methods like "just in time," because we can predict what will be happening.

The importance of routine behavior is recognized in the Six Action Shoes framework, in which the navy formal shoe represents drills, routines, and fixed procedures.

I would guess that more than 90 percent of our lives are governed by established routines and patterns. Certainly 100 percent of our perceptions are.

Where do the patterns come from? There are certain formal procedures that are laid down, and we learn them. When we learn a foreign language we learn the procedures and grammar of that language. When we join an organization, we learn the procedures of that organization or bureaucracy.

Then there are the patterns that we establish for ourselves through personal experience. As any baby grows up, he or she establishes personal patterns, as well as learns already-established patterns like language. Similarly, in any business field an executive builds up patterns that establish a "feel" for the field. Sometimes these patterns can be consciously expressed. At other times, the patterns are not conscious at all, but are expressed as a gut feeling or intuition.

It is difficult, however, to express intuition, hunches, or gut feelings in a serious business discussion. It is for this reason that I assigned a place to feelings in the six hat method that I developed some years ago (*Six Thinking Hats*. New York: Little Brown, 1986). The red hat allows a person to put forward feelings without any need to justify them.

"Putting on my red hat this is what I feel about what we are doing...."

The value of being familiar with a field is that both the explicit and hidden patterns are available and applicable, and they cover most situations. It is also possible, however, to become trapped within these familiar patterns. That is where a certain kind of creative innocence comes in. A person who does not have these established patterns can see something in a fresh way. That is also why industries that have tradition ally been inward looking (particularly the auto industry and retailing) are slow to change. A person within the field can never have the freshness of innocence, so creativity has to be obtained in a different way—through the deliberate escape from fixed patterns by using some of the specific methods of lateral thinking discussed here.

2. Information

If we are driving along a road, a signpost tells us which way to go. A map can also help. The speedometer tells us how fast we are going, while the fuel gauge tells us how much fuel we have. Signposts can tell us how many more miles there are to our destination. In a few cases, a radio broadcast can tell us the state of the traffic up ahead. So we use all of this information to guide us to where we want to go, as well as for feedback on how we are doing. Without this information we are quite simply lost.

Information is the oxygen of business. Without oxygen there is no life. Without information, a business is dead or dying. It is no wonder that we have, so rightly, put major emphasis on access to information. Computers and telecommunications have allowed us to collect, store, sort and distribute information. If we know exactly how much of a part we are using and when we need it, then we can have 'just in time' deliveries. If not, we have to store a large number of parts so that there will be enough to cover our possible needs.

Information is the basis for any decision. We need to know available options. We need to know the consequences of taking any of the options. As we drive along a road, we need to know where we might find lodging for the night. If we know of a better motel up the road, then we need not stop at the first one we see. If we know of a restaurant with better prices, then we can make a better choice.

If we know that the demographic patterns are going to show aging baby boomers, then we might consider getting into the nursing home business. If we know that fewer people are eating meat, then we might prefer to serve pizzas instead of hamburgers.

In the 'six hats' framework the 'white hat' is specifically allocated to information. So when you ask for white hat thinking you are asking those present to restrict their comments purely to information:

"It is time we had some white hat thinking on this . . . ."

In most cases, the idea comes first, and then we use all the information to help us with the idea. If I want to drive to a certain town, then all the information on direction, signposts, and maps help me do that. If I have the idea of lodging for the night, then I seek information to help me with that. If I want to control expenditure in a department or to cut costs, then I seek information to help me with that. If I want to see what new markets are developing, I look to the demographic data to help me with that.

But what about the other way around? Do ideas come from information? Traditionally, in science and elsewhere, we have been taught to analyze information in order to extract ideas. We are now beginning to realize that this is not very effective. If we analyze data, we can see certain correlations like the relationship between cigarette smoking and lung cancer. If we analyze data we can also check out possible ideas that we already have in mind: for example, does the threat of war raise or lower the dollar? But the analysis of data by itself does not generate ideas. We have to have those ideas already in our minds. If there are to be new ideas, we have to start them off in our minds—and the mind can only see what it is prepared to see.

Figure 4.1 shows a series of funnels which represent the patterns already established in our minds by the self-organizing nature of human perception. Whatever we see can only be perceived through these patterns. To perceive a new idea, we have to speculate, imagine, or hypothesize it first. That is why the best scientists now realize that science is as much poetry as data analysis.

Some recent data analysis suggests that drinking decaffeinated coffee is slightly more dangerous than drinking normal coffee from the point of view of heart disease. We could take this at face value or imagine a reason for the choice of decaffeinated coffee in the first place. Perhaps people with a family history of heart trouble or with high blood pressure choose to drink decaffeinated coffee—so the higher incidence of trouble is not surprising. But we have to imagine this possibility first, and then go and check it out. It could even be that people who choose decaffeinated coffee are the more anxious and health-conscious types, and their very anxiety makes them more prone to heart disease.

The Four Wheels of Human Thinking

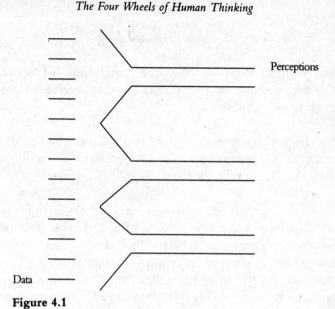

Perceptions

Data

Figure 4.1

Raw information is nothing without the background concepts that allow us to make use of that information. To focus on information without focusing on concepts is to do only half the job.

In a previous section, I mentioned some of the defects of our love of information. I illustrated that information improved our decisions, but that more and more information has a decreasing value (see Figure 1.3). It is at this point that we need new concepts. Once the new concept is there, we can again start to benefit from further information.

I shall be considering in more detail the relationship between information and concepts in the next section.

3. Analysis and Logic

Analysis and logic are the traditional tools of conscious thinking, and almost all our education is focused on getting better at using these tools.

A child with a rash is brought to a doctor. The doctor asks the child to open her mouth. Immediately he recognizes a characteristic Koplik spot and diagnoses measles.

If we can recognize a situation, then we can snap into a reaction pattern. Sometimes we may have to pause to consider how the standard reaction pattern will work under special circumstances. For example, it might be normal for a bank to foreclose on a defaulted mortgage, but in a time of recession and fallen real-estate sales it might not be the best thing to do.

If we cannot recognize a situation, either because it is unknown to us or because there is confusion, then we have to analyze that situation. We seek to break down the situation into parts that we do recognize and can deal with. A chemist will set out to analyze a substance into its component parts. A stock analyst will seek to analyze a company's behavior in order to assess its impact on the value of that company.

Analysis is simplifying, breaking down things into parts, picking out strands and elements. Analysis is comparing unknown things with things that are known. Analysis also involves picking out relationships and putting them back together as a whole.

If there is inflation, do people save or spend more? You could analyze the situation and say that people know that money is going to lose its value, so they turn it into goods, which are a better store of value. So people should spend because it is pointless to save. In fact, in many countries people do save. Why? Because they believe that if basic goods like food are going to cost more, they had better have some savings in order to pay the higher prices. We then find that there are many other factors involved: the history of inflation in that country, inflationary expectations, indexation of wages with inflation, the economic sophistication of the people and journalists, the size of families, and others.

Analysis breaks down when we are dealing with complex systems with many interactive loops. In such systems, you cannot just isolate the parts and put them back together, because in isolating the parts you change the system. The system has to be considered as a whole. So we try to use conceptual models, which are a sort of hypothesis of what may be happening. The difficulty is that in systems with positive feedback loops, a slight change in the parameters at some point may make the system behave in a totally different way. We have to conclude that human thinking simply cannot cope with complex systems of this sort. While computer-modeling of complex systems does help, we nevertheless have to put in the points, connections, relationships, and parameters.

The recent interest of mathematics in non-linear and self-organizing systems is a recognition that the world is much more complex than had been previously thought. Biologists have had to deal with such systems for a long time. Chaos theory, for example, is a somewhat ponderous effort to deal with basic biological organizational structures. With such systems, we come again to the huge importance of concepts and speculation. We have to be able to imagine possibilities. Why does the system behave in this way? We have to imagine possibilities and connections.

Analysis is going to get ever more complex. Increasingly, we are being forced to develop simplifying conceptual models and to use these to guide behavior. The pragmatic value of these models becomes more relevant than their truth. A good example of such a model is medical practice. A doctor deals with a complex system in which much is unknown. Nevertheless, the doctor has to take practical action based on some working hypothesis. Tests are used to provide the basis for the hypothesis, as well as to check it out. Treatment itself becomes a sort of test.

Everyone has heard of "analysis paralysis," which happens when the complexity of interacting possibilities that cannot be checked destroys the basis for confident action. It is at this point that the pragmatism of a doctor needs to take over. This involves action, trying things out, having fallback positions, and being prepared to change direction as you go along.

In the financial world, as in other parts of business, there are people who seem very successful and then suddenly things start to go wrong, and they are heard of no more. What has happened is that such people have a simple conceptual model of the world around them. When this model fits the market conditions, they are very successful; but when the model does not fit, the success is no longer there. This may come about because the model only fits certain conditions or because a model that was accurate at the time is no longer accurate, since other factors have changed the market.

In some ways, logic is the opposite of analysis. Logic seeks to take different things and put them together in order to get a result. If you work upwards from principles or axioms, you may reach a conclusion. Logic is based on the principle that if A is so, then B will follow. Traditional verbal logic is based very much on the principle of contradiction which holds that two mutually exclusive statements cannot both be true. This is a recession. This is not a recession.

In classic logic both these statements cannot be true. Practice, however, is rather different.

The situation might have the feel of a recession, but not the technical characteristics—it might be called a psychological recession.

We might say it really seems like a recession, but if we refuse to call it that, then the self-fulfilling prophecy will not start to work.

We might say that it is borderline whether or not it is a recession and depends on where you are standing.

We might say it is a recession in certain parts of the country, but not in others.

We might even say that it is borderline; you can pick whatever description you want, and you will be right.

The business environment depends so heavily on circumstances, perceptions, anticipatory and competitive behavior, and feedback loops that predictions based on classic logic are very likely to be badly wrong.

Instead of classic verbal logic, which is fine for lawyers, accountants, and engineers, we need to move more towards the non-Western Japanese style. We feed in a lot of information about the situation and gradually build up a sort of mental map or feeling. We then look at the terrain and make our decisions. This is what I have called "water logic," as opposed to traditional "rock logic." Water logic is fluid and flowing, gradually building up. It is not based on choices between permanent, hard-edged, rock-like alternatives.

In my experience, one of the great dangers of traditional logic is the quick use of the negative. As soon as an idea is suggested, there are people who rush to say that it won't work, can't be done, or is too expensive. They then proceed with those bland ideas which survived this instant negativity.

Imagine that there are two sorts of animals. The first might be a grazing animal with plenty of food around. This animal is programmed to react to every noise in the bush as if it might be potential danger (which it often is). The second is a hunting animal. This animal is programmed to react to every noise in the bush as if it were potential prey and food—and is therefore interested in exploring rather than running away.

Too many executives are complacent grazing animals only too ready to shy away from new ideas.

Nevertheless caution, judgement and negativity have a very important place. That is why they are assigned the 'black hat' in six hat thinking.

"We have had a look at the potential of the idea—now we need some thorough black hat thinking."

4. Creativity

In some of my books, I have claimed that humor is the most significant behavior of the human mind. This is a simple statement of fact and is not meant to be provocative.

Humor can only occur in self-organizing information systems which settle down in one stable state and then suddenly reconfigure into another. This reconfiguration is characteristic of self-organizing systems. So the importance of humor is that it indicates, more directly than anything else, that the human mind works as a self-organizing system. The fact that traditional philosophers, psychologists, and even information theorists have paid so little attention to humor is because they have all been looking at passive or externally-organized information systems. In such passive systems, humor cannot occur—so they ignored it. Our recent insights into self-organizing systems, however, now allow us to see the significance of humor.

Creativity is based on the same process as humor. The time sequence of experience sets up certain patterns of perception, certain ways of looking at things. There are side patterns (as shown in Figure 4.2), but we cannot get access to them. If suddenly we do get access to the side pattern, then we have either humor or creativity. Designing ways of helping us to move across patterns is the basis of lateral thinking which will be introduced in a later section of the book. The word "lateral" is derived from moving sideways across patterns.

Every valuable creative idea must always be logical in hindsight. If it were not, we would never be able to see its value. It would simply be a crazy idea. The idea might indeed be crazy forever or until we caught up with it. Consider the following two ideas:

if a plastic piece is not strong enough, make it thinner, and

if you want to increase sales, raise the price.

It is difficult to accept these as valuable ideas since they are not immediately logical in hindsight. With a little more thought, however, both can be seen as logical.

Because we have assumed that every valuable idea must always be logical in hindsight, we have never paid serious at-

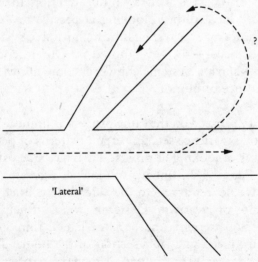

Figure 4.2

tention to creativity. We have assumed that if an idea is logical in hindsight, then better logic should have been able to reach it in the first place. We now know that in self-organizing information systems, this reasoning is totally wrong. In any self-organizing system, creativity is absolutely essential.

In practice, very few people know or accept that creativity is a logical necessity. Most dismiss the matter by asking for examples of creativity, and then show that these examples (in hindsight) are simply plain logic.

Even those who do see a value in creativity believe its use should be restricted to product design, packaging, promotion, and other extraneous matters. This is a dangerous fallacy.

There is an absolute need for creativity in all thinking that involves perceptions and concepts, and there is very little thinking that does not involve perceptions and concepts. In finance, engineering, and science, there is every bit as much need for creative thinking as in product design. It is one of the great failures of our education system to assume that creative thinking is confined to the arts and is not part of the hard sciences.

If we cannot use creativity, we cannot use much of the potential available in our knowledge, our experience, and our assets. In fact, creativity is the cheapest and best way of getting added value from existing assets.

There are those who recognize the importance of creativity, but still believe that nothing can or need be done about it. Such people believe that ideas will happen from time to time and that some people happen to be creative, while others are not. This is a passive attitude that is no longer tenable. We can do a lot to develop creative thinking attitudes and methods in everybody.

As a way of making time and space available for creative effort there is the 'green hat' in the six hat system. This makes it possible at a meeting to ask specifically for new ideas.

"Green hat thinking now. What new alternatives are there?"

(The six hats system has proved so practical and convenient that it has been taken up by many major corporations. For example, in 1990 IBM used it as the core of its training for 40,000 managers world-wide.)

5

Concepts and Information

What is a concept? It is almost impossible to define—and almost not worth trying. But I recognize concepts, look for them, design them, and use them.

Furthermore, there is a distinction between a concept and an idea. An idea is something specific that you can carry out. A concept is a more general, abstract notion that has to be carried out by means of a specific idea. For example, traveling along a road is a concept, but in practice, you have to do something specific such as walk, ride a bicycle, or drive a car.

Contrary to our normal thinking, concepts are often more useful when they are blurred, vague, and fuzzy, because then they have more potential. If they are too detailed, they cover too little. If they are too general, they cover too much and provide little direction. In time, a creative thinker gets a feeling for when a concept is specific enough, yet general enough at the same time.

There is little distinction between a concept and a perception. When we look out at the world we never see raw data. The data we receive has already been organized into patterns by previous experience (the self-organizing nature of the mind). A person born blind who suddenly becomes able to see cannot see. That person has to learn to see and to build up usable patterns. This organization into patterns, sequences, or groups we call perception. Figure 4.1 suggests how we group certain things together to obtain perceptions.

So a perception is a grouping of things realized when we look out at the world. A concept is a grouping of things realized when we look inwardly at our available experience.

When we have grouped things into a perception, we often put a name on that grouping: a flower, a mountain, a restaurant.

When we have grouped things into a concept, there is a purpose or benefit that arises from the grouping: sales tax, traffic control, a restaurant franchise.

A restaurant is both a description and a concept; it sells people food and is a place to eat it. The purpose and benefit are obvious.

The Benetton Corporation was started less than twenty years ago by two brothers and a sister in Italy. One brother was a minor accountant, and the sister was a seamstress in a garment factory. Today, Benetton is worth about $2 billion—

and this is in a very crowded industry with tremendous competition. So how did it all happen? There were a number of concepts that helped.

The first was to sell color, not shape. Colors are easy to display, and are not as dependent on fashion as shape. Colors can be changed.

So most of the garments were made without color. Those that were colored were put out in shops. If red appeared to be selling well, then the garments were dyed red. If green was selling, then the garments were dyed green.

The usual pattern in the garment industry follows two lines. Either this is what has always sold, so let us stick to it; or this is what we believe people will want, so let us persuade them to buy it as this season's fashion.

The Benetton concept was both reactive and flexible. This sort of immediate reactivity is common in the mail order business, but it was new in the garment industry. Flexibility, as everyone knows, is now one of the key trends in business anywhere.

Another concept was to start with jumpers, sweaters, pullovers, cardigans, and other semi-premium, high-margin items. Such items would best show color. They were also very traditional items without much innovation. Later, Benetton opened up a wider range of products.

In addition, instead of having to go through store buyers (what would buyers have bought, anyway?), Benetton opened up its own stores with very simple layout and design. Today there are about 6,000 stores worldwide. This allows direct access to the public and instant feedback.

Finally, there was a high degree of automation and computer control. For example, a warehouse handling about 500,000 items a day only had six people involved. All these concepts put together led to success in a very difficult field.

The Body Shop has also been a successful retailing concept. Since people were becoming health and environmentally conscious, the corporation focused on natural products. Putting together body-treatment products separately from the usual drug and pharmaceutical context also had a positive effect. Finally there was a great deal of skill in carrying through the concept with design, colors, and sound organization. This is a good example of the "integrated value" aspect that I will consider later. Any successful concept always consists of two parts: the concept and its implementation.

KLM airlines in Holland had the problem with the population of its home base. It was very small compared to that of other airlines crossing the Atlantic (USA, UK, Germany, France, etc.). So KLM developed the successful concept of "feeder" airlines. By running flights to lesser cities in Germany and England, KLM pulled passengers away from their own national airlines. At one time KLM was flying more Germans across the Atlantic than Lufthansa, the country's national airline.

Henry C. Yuen and Daniel S. Kwoh invented the VCR Plus to provide a convenience value (one of the most important driving values). Instead of having to cope with different and complex systems, all you had to do was punch in a code and the VCR would record at the right time. Gemstar Development Corporation now generates the code numbers and sells them to newspapers. In time, when VCR's incorporate the technology directly, the coding system will provide the revenue.

The Wright brothers were the first to fly because they changed the base concept. They did not start off with any superior technology. All those working on flying machines knew that curved wings would provide lift, and they all had access to gasoline engines that would drive propellers. But most designers were seeking to design a stable plane. They had experimented with hand-launched models that had to maintain their balance as they flew through the air, so "stability" became the design objective, and designers tried harder and harder in that direction. The contribution of the Wright brothers changed this direction; they became interested in "unstable" flying machines. This meant that sooner or later one wing would dip down. Unless they could bring that wing up, the plane would crash. So they now focused their attention and experimentation on how to bring up the dipped wing. They found that by twisting or warping the wing, they could increase lift on one side and decrease it on another. They developed controls. They became the first to fly. Much later on, inherently stable planes were developed. Today, fighter planes have to be made deliberately unstable, otherwise they are too slow to maneuver.

The great civilizations of Egypt, Greece, and Rome were unable to measure time effectively. They had the technology—water clocks, hour glasses, and other instruments—but they did not have the concept. They were trying to divide the day into twelve equal hours and the night, quite separately, into another twelve equal hours. Since this was being done in the Mediterranean, day and night varied in length throughout the year (June 21 was the longest day and December 21 the longest night). Trying to divide varying quantities into equal amounts is not easy. It was only in the thirteenth century that Arabian mathematician Abu L'Hassan came up with the idea of measuring a day from the sun's peak on one day to its peak (midday) on the next day, and then dividing this into twenty-four hours. It was not until 1863 that the Japanese realized the value of this new concept.

Concepts are extremely important, but very difficult to generate. In hindsight, of course, almost all successful concepts seem easy and obvious.

In my seminars I often put a heavy steel ball on the surface of the overhead projector and then ask the audience to think of a practical barrier that I could put on the projector to stop the ball from rolling forward. The use of hands is disallowed, and the barrier must be practical and available in the room. Three broad types of suggestion usually emerge:

1. The concept of heaviness: some barrier that would be heavy enough to absorb the energy of the ball, such as books, a briefcase, or shoes.
2. The concept of fixity: a barrier should be taped down on the surface of the projector and so resist the motion of the ball. The barrier need not be heavy.
3. The concept of resistance: some sticky stuff or double-sided tape could be used to increase rolling resistance and bring the ball to a halt.

Concepts and Information

I then show a different concept of a barrier. This is a piece of folded paper as shown in Figure 5.1. This barrier is so light that it can be blown away with a puff of breath. Yet it serves to halt the ball. Rolling onto the paper, the ball itself creates a barrier, as shown in the figure. This barrier is not necessarily any better the ones previously suggested, for to judge merit you have to know exact specifications and needs. But it is a different concept—that of getting the ball to stop itself.

Forming Concepts

In a later section I shall be dealing more specifically with the generation and design of concepts. What I want to do here is to explore the relationship between information and concepts.

Imagine a number of balls dropping randomly onto a tray of sand. The balls remain where they have been dropped, as in Figure 5.2. Now imagine that the receiving surface is not sand, but a ridged structure as shown in Figure 5.3. The balls will always end up in parallel rows no matter where the starting position might have been. It is exactly the same with perception. We can only only receive information in the patterns that have already been formed.

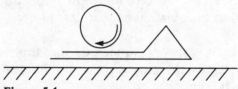

Figure 5.1

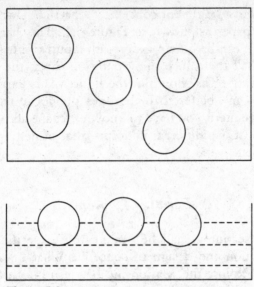

Figure 5.2

So the analysis of information is unlikely to form concepts. In practice this is not strictly true, because if you read in a paper that the Soviet Union is very short of eyeglasses and then read elsewhere of a growing thirst for vodka, you might develop the idea of selling eyeglasses to the Soviet Union and being paid in vodka. So the examination of information does allow us to form simple concepts or to select from concepts which we already have. But we are very unlikely to form new concepts, unless we have somehow started them first in our minds with imagination or speculation.

That is why it is so vital to increase the emphasis on creative and conceptual thinking in education. Information analysis will not be enough.

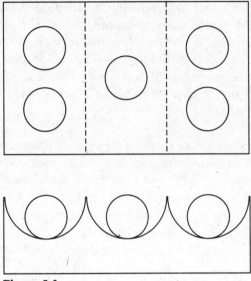

Figure 5.3

A concept may start with a simple wish. At one time, I was giving a seminar to senior executives in Goodwill Industries, which seeks to sell at low cost clothes and materials which have been donated to it. It seemed to me that if they had more stuff to sell or a wider range of choice, they would do better. How could one persuade people to donate more?

Then came what I call a "provocation." If people were not willing to give more, then why not go and take it? While it seemed to be getting pretty close to burglary, from that provocation came the concept of a "clearing out service." Many people accumulate a lot of junk which they never get around to clearing out. Even if they wished to clear it out, they did not know where to put it. I suggested that Good Will should mark what it wanted to retain with a red sticker, and then invite the clear out service to remove everything else, thus providing a service for the customer and a source of materials for itself. This use of provocation is part of the creative thinking process I will discuss in a later section.

The modification or improvement of existing concepts and the revival of older concepts is another means of forming new concepts. In 1991 the sales from warehouse clubs are expected to rise 28 percent to $28 billion. Customers pay a membership fee of $25, which mainly serves to give them a psychological stake in shopping at the outlets. Then there is discount shopping in bulk, which also means that the club must buy in bulk in order to give the lowest prices. The concept is an old one, but it fits recession psychology. The new angle may be the club and membership idea. The customer wants to get value from the membership, so he buys at the warehouse to begin with. Once the habit is established, then the habit continues.

A good example of the revival of older concepts is Commodore Business Machines. Like many other such companies, Commodore found servicing to be expensive. So it passed over servicing to a new division of Federal Express called Business Logistics Services, which collects the machines, drops off replacements, and even repairs the machines at centralized points. Courier services were a powerful concept in their day (and still are), but the advent of the fax machine reduced their growth. So there has been a need for new "old" concepts, such as the Business Logistics service. In time, physical handling will become obsolete, and servicing will be done by a combination of telephone line diagnostics and modular-plug replacements.

We may look at some retail sales figures and find that people over 60 are not spending much money. What does that mean? Does it mean that we should avoid building retail outlets in areas with aging populations? Does it mean that older people do not have money to spend? Does it mean that they are unwilling to spend money? Or, could it mean that at the moment there is nothing for them to spend their money on? Perhaps there is a lack of attractive goods designed for the seniors market. Perhaps people have money, but are uncertain of their future medical requirements. So there might be an opportunity for different types of insurance. There might also be an opportunity for reverse mortgages which unlock the capital value of residences so that the money can be used during a person's lifetime. So we see that a simple piece of information can give rise to many concepts. But the concepts come from our own minds.

Children's books often contain a simple puzzle in which there are many fishermen and a tangle of lines. On one of the lines, a fish is hooked. The child is asked to find out which fisherman has hooked the fish. If you start off with the fisherman, the task is quite hard, because you have no way of telling which line leads to the fish. If you start off with the fish then all you have to do is to follow the line back to the fisherman. What could be easier?

It is the same with concepts. They are obvious in hindsight, so logical and so related to existing information, that we believe that we could easily have gotten them by analyzing the information.

Concept and Context

What is the significance of the color red?

In terms of traffic lights, it means stop.

In a political sense red means Communist.

As purely a color, red is one of the primary ones.

In the context of wine, red is the one that has tannin.

It all depends on the context.

Data only becomes information when it is put into or viewed in a context. The context may be a set of circumstances or the context may be a concept.

In American supermarkets, 80 percent of purchases are said to be on impulse. In considering ways of increasing this impulse buying, you could look at traffic flow, eye levels, where people pause, whether customers can go straight to the shelves they want, and a variety of other factors. Things which are not significant in one context can become significant in another.

Sometimes an anomaly or a blip in the data can arouse suspicion and even trigger a concept. Then we must look at the data through that concept.

The important point, which I keep repeating, is the need to do conceptual work in our head and not just wait for information to provide us with concepts—because it will not.

6

Sur/petition versus Competition

Competition is for survival.

Sur/petition is for success.

Competition is the key ingredient in free-market economics. It prevents monopoly pricing and ensures that consumers get the best deal. It ensures that producers make every effort to be efficient and to provide quality. If not, they risk being driven out of business by a producer who offers better prices or better quality.

The purpose of competition is to benefit the consumer by keeping prices down and quality up. Competition also benefits the economy as a whole by ensuring the most efficient use of resources and encouraging enterprise. Newcomers with better ideas, prices, or quality can enter the field and compete against those already in it. There is, then, a great deal to be said for competition.

But competition is designed for the benefit of the economy as a whole and for the consumer. Only part of the benefit of competition is for the producers. To be sure, producers are driven to greater productivity and efficiency, but the benefits of this are not reflected in greater profits, only in survival. If two people are tugging at the end of a rope, a huge amount of effort on both sides does not mean that the rope will move. Organizations may put a lot of effort into competing with one another, but the end result may be merely the same existing market share for each. It is true, however, that competition allows the more effective producer to increase market share at the expense of the less efficient producer. Sales volume may go up, but margins and profits may not.

In short, competition puts pressure on producers. You have to be competitive in order to survive. Just as labor costs and environmental concerns are pressures on producers, so also is competition.

Competition is necessary for maintenance and to ensure the baseline of survival.

Sur/petition, on the other hand, is concerned with how you move upwards from that baseline. Physical monopolies are illegal in many countries, but value monopolies are not. Value monopolies are for the benefit of the producers, and are also in the interests of consumers. Most developed countries have moved away from survival economics, in fact, and toward value economics. Value economics means that consumers can choose what value means most for them. You do not need a video cassette in order to survive. You choose a particular one because that is the value you want. You can choose to spend $1,000 on a Rolex watch because you value something about it. From a survival point of view, you could get just as good time-keeping from a Timex.

In today's value economics, sur/petition and value monopolies are very much in the general economic interest. Without value monopolies, all would be commodity economics. There would be nowhere to spend money and no point in earning it. That is precisely what went wrong with the economy in the Soviet Union; people had money but nowhere to spend it, except on low-priced commodities. Value economics is concerned with creating opportunities for spending money as you wish.

So value economics, sur/petition, and value monopolies are good for the economy, for consumers, and for producers. This is in contrast to competition, which mainly benefits the economy and consumers. Classic competition certainly needs to be there, otherwise the benefits of value economics will quickly disappear. But once classic competition is in place, it is no longer sufficient. We also need sur/petition in order to make value economics work.

On a visit to Japan I had a long discussion with Masaru Ibuka, who was the real founder of Sony (Akio Morita came in a bit later). Ibuka started making tape recorders immediately after the war. It is difficult to be certain about the real story of the origin of the Sony Walkman because hindsight changes most stories, but I suspect it was quite simple. There was probably a suggestion that the tape recorder should be made much smaller—perhaps the size of a book. I doubt very much indeed, however, that there was any concept of the Walkman as such. It is simply a very natural tendency for the Japanese to want to make things smaller. They live in a crowded country (with a population of over 100 million, Japan is about the size of the state of Montana), often in very small apartments. Everything has to be miniaturized. Added to this is the Japanese propensity for things to be delicate and exquisite—as in the serving of a Japanese meal. So there was simply a tendency to make a smaller tape recorder, as there is with all products today. That was all.

Suddenly it became obvious that the small tape recorder was now small enough to be carried around. However, this was not an obvious value in Japan. Why should anyone want to carry a tape recorder around? But the portable tape recorder then snapped into powerful "integrated values" of the United States.

A generation brought up on watching television 30 hours a week was in need of constant stimulation. Habits of internal stimulation (such as thinking) had never been developed. Without external stimulation, the brain was inactive. Thus the portable tape recorder provided the ideal means of providing stimulation wherever you went.

In this way, the great success of the Sony Walkman came about. The name itself was even a particular success, although if you examine it closely, there is no indication whatever of either music or its function. The real contribution of Sony was not in devising the Walkman, which I believe came about unintentionally, but rather in recognizing its potential success and running with it. Further, Sony did not sit back and relish its success. It started producing model after model. Today, Sony is still the leader in the field, with revenues from the Walkman of about $150 million a year. There are over one hundred other competitors offering very similar models, but Sony is still the leader.

The way Sony handled its success is the real lesson. Too many Western companies with an initial success like the Walkman would not have known how to follow it up (after all, Philips invented the VCR and made absolutely nothing of it). Western companies would have been pleased with success and determined to make the most of it before competitors jumped in and destroyed the value monopoly. That is precisely why many companies have been disillusioned with innovation. They claim that they put in the development costs and open up the market, and then the "me-too" operators jump in and take all the profits. This is indeed what happens if you sit back. Once it got started on the Walkman, Sony did not sit back, but rushed to get out second- and third-generation models even while the first model was still profitable.

Sony established sur/petition with the Walkman by a combination of initial concept (however this came about) and vigorous follow-through. Sony created its own race—which is what sur/petition is all about.

Value Monopolies

There are a number of traditional ways in which value monopolies have been established in the past. Some of them are still as important as they ever were, while others have become less important.

Physical Uniqueness

There is only one Mona Lisa. There is only one Van Gogh
'Irises'. There are three things that are important in building a
hotel: location, location, and location. There are prime sites,
and if you have a prime site you have a value monopoly.
Prime sites can and do change in value; for example, many
grand old hotels where built near railway stations—hardly a
prime site today.

I own a private island in Venice. There is only one Venice
in the world—the world's most beautiful city by far. There
can never be another Venice. The island is the only private
island on the main waterway from the airport into Venice.
This means that the island is accessible at all conditions of
tide. This is unique.

The art business and the antiques business are built on
physical uniqueness. The value of artworks tends to fluctu-
ate because they get overblown at times and then collapse
in order to start the cycle all over again—to the benefit of
dealers who can never thrive in a static market.

Technological Uniqueness

Most people know of the $600 million settlement which
Polaroid obtained against Kodak for infringement of their
patents on instant film. Patents are an obvious example of
value monopoly. The emphasis of the courts in the United
States has swung recently much more in favor of patent holders. At one time, the mood was that patent holders were ex-
tortionists obstructing free competition. But along with the
rise of the Far East economies, there arose a realization that

intellectual property is important and should be protected. There was, for instance, successful pressure on Singapore to clean up the video copying industry that used to thrive there.

The pharmaceutical industry ($57 billion in the United States) is perhaps the most favored by patent protection and technological uniqueness. A new drug may cost $231 million to develop. The pharmaceutical industry spends 16.8 percent of sales on research, a sum that amounts to $8.2 billion or almost twice the total of the American film industry. It is in everyone's interest that new drugs be developed, so it is only appropriate that this huge investment in research be rewarded. Countries like Italy, which do not allow drug patents, consequently never develop new drugs. There are approximately seventeen years of patent life for every drug. The FDA uses the first ten years in trials and testings. That leaves seven profitable years for a company to recoup its investment and to pay for future research. In even this short period, many pharmaceutical companies reap huge rewards.

The peptic ulcer treatment drugs, for example, were huge successes. Mevacor, from the Merck Corporation, is designed to lower cholesterol and will probably reach $1.5 billion in sales world-wide. Proscar, used for prostate treatment and also from Merck, probably will be a big winner. Cognex from Warner Lambert, used in the treatment of Alzheimer's disease, has huge potential.

Outside the pharmaceutical field, sur/petition through technology is much less assured. One year when I was giving a talk at the World Economic Forum in Davos, I happened to attend a talk given by Colby Chandler, who was then chief executive of Kodak. Kodak is hardly a slouch at technology, yet he said that technology was fast becoming a common commodity. At best there is only a six month to one year lead available through technology. State of the art scientific development will soon make technology available to everyone.

I remember talking to the members of the research department of a large chemical company and discussing future research. It was possible, they said, to produce better and better materials and better and better fibers. But the market for very specialized and high-quality materials was very small. Why spend millions on research to have a market that was limited to the nose cones of rockets?

To some extent this phenomenon is happening with American microchip makers. Instead of competing head-on with the powerful Japanese chip makers, Americans are retiring from the commodity chip business, and focusing on special designs and applications. This certainly protects margins, but it also locks them out from the large-volume markets of appliances and other things which are going to be the big users of chips. You can keep your margins, but you also progressively reduce your market.

The lesson of the Sony Walkman is applicable here. There was miniaturization, but no great technological breakthrough. The value of the Walkman was obtained by an application concept. In the future, therefore, application concepts are going to be far more valuable than pure technology. That is why there is a need to treat concept development as seriously as technical development. That is why, in a later section,

I shall be advocating setting up serious Concept R&D departments. The second lesson from the Sony Walkman was its marketing and follow-through. It is not enough to build a superior mousetrap and then sit back and wait for people to beat a path to your door.

Name Recognition

There is a whole industry in Agatha Christie films and videos. The designer industry is based on individuals with moderate good taste, slick marketing, and image-hungry consumers. Whether it is Reebok, Lacroix, Gucci, or Calvin Klein, there are people and names. Books by popular authors or films with well-known stars are all in the people uniqueness area of sur/petition.

Hollywood and the music industry are special examples of American sur/petition. The large home market and American hype have created stars which are saleable throughout the world. Overseas sales now account for 42 percent of Hollywood studio income. There is a worldwide demand for American stars like Michael Jackson and Madonna.

While the Japanese may dominate the listening and viewing end of the entertainment business, the United States has dominated the software or input end. The Japanese know this, so Sony bought Columbia and Matsushita bought MCA to have access to all the software rights that have accumulated. Only three of the major U.S. studios are now in American hands. But regardless of who controls it, name recognition is a very powerful form of sur/petition because it is difficult to dislodge.

Dominance

Occasionally a corporation gets into a position that is so dominant that it provides sur/petition by virtue of the position alone. This is certainly true in the case of Boeing, which dominates the aircraft industry. A succession of sound models, and in particular the very successful 747, has given Boeing this position. The order books are full for years ahead. There is growing competition from Airbus Industrie, but this company has a long way to go. Down the road, there may well emerge a powerful competitor based on USSR plane technology supplemented by German and Japanese advanced technology. The Russians certainly know about planes. Aeroflot is probably the busiest airline in the world, and Soviet military aircraft are highly developed.

IBM still has a dominant share in the computer industry, but it has slipped. In mainframes there is now hot competition from Amdahl, Fujitsu, and Hitachi. In other areas, clones are making inroads. Furthermore, IBM's cost per sale is higher than that of many smaller competitors. Much computer technology is now at commodity prices. IBM was a bit behind on the concepts of connectivity and network concepts.

A dominant position is a good base for sur/petition, one can conclude, but needs to be used. In fact, a dominant position is always much more vulnerable than it looks. I suspect that Boeing is already becoming somewhat complacent about its dominant position.

Another example, AT&T, still has a dominant position, even though it is not as strong as it used to be. The introduction of the AT&T charge card, with discounts on long distance calls, however, is a good example of integrated values. In fact, about seven years ago I was giving a seminar to Bell Canada in Toronto and mentioned that telephone companies were in an ideal position to get into financial services.

Cost of Entry

CMOS chips require less power than normal chips, but require heavy capital investment. Because they use less power, they are useful in laptop computers, which are mostly made in Japan.

Where the cost of entry is high and requires a continuous injection of development funds, there is protection from newcomers. There has to be existing cash flow, however, to cover these development costs. This is particularly difficult in the United States, where quarterly stock-analyst reports impose a much shorter investment horizon than in Japan.

Once something is established, the cost of displacing it may be huge. For example, the QWERTY keyboard was designed to slow down typing so that the mechanical keys of the early typewriters did not jam. The continuance of that layout of keys meant that more and more typists learned on it, so makers produced that kind of keyboard. Today we could design a much more efficient one, but the cost of introducing it would be huge.

It is sometimes the same with getting people to change their eating habits. No one has succeeded in selling ice cream to the French. Yet other foods are accepted quite easily.

Brand Image

The most traditional way of getting some sort of value monopoly is through the brand image. McDonald's does very well in spite of its many competitors. Heinz tomato ketchup continues to be a favorite. Familiarity, availability, dependability and general image are important when other values are similar. Brand images are always threatened by private labels from retailers, by the way in which retailers in many countries squeeze margins, and by the insistence of retailers on doing their own advertising. Advertisers are going to find it increasingly difficult to suggest real value differences among many competing products. Perhaps the main value of brand-image advertising is circular. Retailers stock the product because they feel consumers will demand it. Because the product is stocked, consumers buy it, thus justifying the retailers' purchase.

Although brand images are a useful way of getting sur/petition, and although there probably is an even greater need for them in the future, I suspect that it will become increasingly difficult to sustain them as quality improves all around and consumers become more and more conscious of real values.

Harvard Business School is a good example of the circularity of brand image. A lot of very bright people come out of Harvard Business School and enhance its reputation. This means that the value of getting there increases, so more people apply. This gives the school a greater range of selection, allowing it to take only the very best. This both enhances its reputation and ensures that its products are of good value. The actual teaching methods there are as irrelevant as an

archway through which a number of highly intelligent people walk. If intelligent people enter the archway, it is no
surprise that equally intelligent people emerge.

Segmentation

While there is overcapacity in retailing and most corporations
are shedding or closing stores, Wayne Badovinus is planning
to open more Eddie Bauer Inc. stores. The secret is that
he is focusing on outdoor and casual wear—which people
are inclined to buy because it is less susceptible to fashion
and therefore longer lasting. He is also focusing on married
couples in their upper forties.

Very specific niches, segmentations, and market focus of
this sort have always been a way of getting sur/petition.
At very least they give a company a good starting position.
Even when others enter the same area, there is still an initial advantage, provided that management can keep up the
quality. The very successful Marks and Spencer retail chain
in the United Kingdom was originally known for selling
middle-income underwear. It then established a position in
good-quality, mid-priced clothing. It used this base to get
into food retailing with its own label products. Today it is
as successful as ever, making more money from food than
from clothing.

As always, there is an initial advantage and then the importance of follow-through. It is possible to have market
segments that are even too specific. There is, then, the same
problem as with very specialized products. The market may
be very small. To have a dominant position in a very small
market may not be good enough. If the market gets bigger

or seems lucrative, others will certainly take a good look at it.

Protection or Plus

I have considered above some of the more traditional methods of getting value monopolies. Some of them are forms of protection, like patents and cost of entry. A few are based on unassailable uniqueness, like special geography or individuals. The rest have to be based on some sort of "plus." Brand image, for example, is a traditional way of promising a plus, and in the past this was a real value in terms of product quality or consistency. Today brand image may be a rather weak form of plus.

The real plus factors are going to come from careful attention to integrated values. Domino's Pizza is based directly on this concept. People who feel like having a pizza do not feel like going out to get one, so Domino's delivers to their door. Pizza Hut and other competitors will start making their own deliveries soon—if they are not doing so already.

Perrier is another good example of integrated values. Perrier introduced the concept of "designer" water and kept up the pressure to remain the market leader. People were becoming more health conscious. President Carter was exhorting people not to have more than two martinis at lunch. So what was the sophisticated person going to drink at lunch? You could not ask for a Coke, because that was for teenagers, and beer was not sophisticated enough. Water made you seem very cheap and often tasted awful. So consumers were crying out for the most expensive possible way of drinking water. Perrier satisfied that need. All at once water became not only socially acceptable, but even a mark of sophistication. As before we need to recognize the initial concept and also the successful follow-through.

Both Kid Cuisine and Snoopy's Choice are attempts to benefit from the integrated value of concern over junk food and sound nutrition. What is offered are nutritiously sound meals attractive to children.

C. R. Eggs of Pennsylvania feeds its chickens on a special diet of rice bran, alfalfa, Vitamin E, and sea kelp. The company claims that in a controlled trial, a group of people on a low-fat and low-cholesterol diet who ate a dozen of these special eggs a week had the same cholesterol levels as those who had the same diet but no eggs. This special integrated value allows the eggs to be sold at a premium of 60 percent.

General Motors is having a hard time competing with Toyota in terms of cost and engineering. In time, GM will probably catch up, but by then the market share may have slumped. Perhaps GM should take a closer look at integrated values. Perhaps GM should get into the car parking business as I had suggested to Ford (UK). Perhaps GM, with its huge financial muscle, should have a guaranteed buy-back price for its cars after every year of use. These cars could then be resold as used vehicles. At present, U.S. fleets account for 10 percent of car sales. The low mileage cars (3000 miles) are bought back and sold to dealers, who could then sell them at a good margin. It seems that buyers of these low-mileage used cars are older and richer than the buyers of new cars. So there is a market for low-mileage used cars.

It might be argued that this would hurt GM's sales of new cars. Perhaps so, but that may not matter. One of the worst reasons for not doing something is that it might hurt existing business (see what happened to the Swiss watch industry in a later section). As I said earlier, a car is not just a lump of engineering. One of the integrated values of a car is its ability to resell at a good price with no hassle. If GM were able to offer a guaranteed buy-back price there would be a considerable incentive to buy GM in the first place. Toyota and others might be hard put to compete in this sort of matter. Billions spent on technical research will not develop this sort of concept. But that is where sur/petition may be found—in new concepts.

The Source of Sur/petition

Sur/petition goes far beyond housekeeping. Getting things right within the organization (cost control, quality) is certainly essential, but this merely gets the baseline right. Classic competition is really part of housekeeping, though it is also concerned with getting the baseline right. Quality and prices have to be right. There is indeed a slight overlap between product differentiation and sur/petition, but the overlap is not large. Sur/petition is not so much concerned with differentiating changes in the product being offered as it is by uniqueness in the value being provided. So when we have distinguished between housekeeping and sur/petition, and are firmly focused on sur/petition, how are we going to make this happen?

Some of the traditional approaches to value monopoly will still hold their importance. These were considered earlier in this section. Some of them can be improved and polished up. But what other sources are there, particularly for the plus aspect of sur/petition?

There are three broad sources:

1. *Integrated values.* At several points in this section and also in preceding sections I have emphasized the growing importance of integrated values as distinct from product values. I intend to consider this whole area of integrated values in much more detail in a later section.

2. *Serious creativity.* Sur/petition is based directly on concepts and ideas. However much information, experience, and decision ability we may have, there is still going to be a huge need for new ideas. Such ideas are not going to be created by analysis or computer sorting of information. They are going to be generated by human creativity. We have to move beyond the crazy view of creativity to focus on serious creativity and how we can use it. It is not enough to hope that the creative people in your advertising agency will provide the ideas you need. This sort of reliance has been largely ineffectual. Serious creativity will also be considered in a later section.

3. *Concept R&D.* Organizations spend millions and billions of dollars on technical research and development. They know that they have to do this in order to survive. In the future, wise organizations are going to learn that they need to treat concept development every bit as seriously as they now treat technical development. Indeed, technology is becoming a commodity, while profits and sur/petition are going to come from application concepts.

So the overall message is that creative and conceptual thinking is going to become ever more important. Every successful organization is going to have a three part strategy:

1. Get the housekeeping right.
2. Develop the concepts for sur/petition.
3. Have an energetic follow-through.

I want to end this section by emphasizing the need for energetic follow through. The best concept in the world has only a limited value (certainly in time) unless there is energetic follow through.

7

Words, Traps, and Dangers

We often forget that the words we develop for the convenience of communication can become dangerous traps which
force us to look at the world in a particular way. We can
only see what we are prepared to see. If we come across
something which is totally new, we pause to consider what
it might be—usually by analyzing it down into fragments
which are familiar. But if we come across something that
seems, at first sight, to be similar to something we know,
then we see it only as this familiar thing and totally fail to
see why it is actually different.

Let me give a very real example of this dangerous habit of
words.

Twenty years ago I pioneered the direct teaching of thinking in schools. The CoRT method is now the most widely
used method internationally for the direct teaching of

thinking as a school subject. In some cases, there are whole countries which have made the teaching of thinking compulsory in every school. Millions of students are involved.

In Venezuela a professor of philosophy at the University of Caracas, Luis Alberto Machado, happened to read my book *The Mechanism of Mind* which was published in Venezuela. The book provided the stimulus for his own thinking and dynamism. He entered politics, and when his party won the elections, he was asked what ministry he would like. He asked for a totally new one: a ministry for the development of intelligence. Later, at a Club of Rome meeting in Salzburg, he asked if anyone present knew me. Publisher Robert Maxwell said he did, and arranged a meeting between myself and Dr. Machado. He told me he had a new ministry, but was not sure what to do next. I told him about the CoRT program. He took it back to Venezuela and had it translated into Spanish. He invited me over, and I trained local teachers (and later teachers in the public and technical institutes). The Venezuelans then set up their own seminars and in four years had trained 105,000 teachers. A law was passed making the teaching of thinking compulsory in all schools. Of the 14 projects in the Ministry of Intelligence, eight were based on my work. Much later on, there was a Harvard project which never really got off the ground before the Venezuelan elections changed governments. About 900 students were trained in the Harvard project, compared to 1.5 million in the CoRT project. I mention this only because the impression given in the United States is somewhat different.

The Venezuelan project was the impetus for the current interest in teaching thinking in schools in the United States.

This movement has become something of a bandwagon onto which publishers and others are jumping without really understanding what it is about.

The movement has been very nearly wrecked by the inappropriate term "critical thinking." When the movement to teach thinking started, older philosophers assumed that thinking must mean critical thinking, because that has been the traditional approach (based on the Greek tradition which I have mentioned before). Critical thinking is based on searching for the truth and asking students to point out errors in what has been placed before them.

This sort of lawyer-type thinking does have a value and should occupy about 20 percent of the attention we pay to thinking. But it is only part of thinking. The extremely important generative, constructive, productive, and creative side of thinking is completely left out. Yet it is precisely this productive thinking that is going to be so important for the economic welfare of a nation. Anyone in business knows that you have to produce. Just describing and criticizing is totally inadequate. You cannot grow a garden just by using pruning shears. The avoidance of error in thinking is not enough. You could, after all, avoid all errors in driving by leaving the car in the garage.

So the movement was taken over by the title "critical thinking." Somehow teachers were embarrassed to say they were teaching "thinking"—there had to be an adjective, and the traditional adjective was "critical."

Critical thinking has a specific and precise meaning. The word critical comes from the Greek "kritikos," which means "to judge." Critical thinking, therefore, means judgment thinking. To be sure, this kind of thinking is very important, but you also have to produce something. Those who claim that critical thinking covers all aspects of thinking are destroying the real value of the word and are leaving judgment thinking without its proper title.

The greatest danger in the current critical-thinking movement is that its advocates claim that critical thinking covers all thinking, but then end up teaching only traditional critical thinking. The whole productive aspect gets left out.

In this way, the inappropriate use of the word "critical" is doing serious damage to the future of American education.

Competition

I am reasonably certain that the gurus of competition will insist that sur/petition is really part of traditional competition, and that it is something they have been advocating all along. I would agree that there have been numerous examples of sur/petition and that the approach of some people to competition is very close to sur/petition. But I also believe that it is very important to make the distinction between competition and sur/petition; otherwise, we cannot give sur/petition the full attention that it deserves. Otherwise we can so easily get the sequence:

" . . . it is really just a part of competition."

" . . . we have been advocating competition for years."

" . . . therefore we need not do anything about it."

There is the very well-known and often-told story of the two boys who are walking through a national park. They encounter a bear who seems about to attack them. One boy suggests they should start to run away. The other boy calmly sits down on the ground and starts to put on his running shoes. The first boy looks at him in amazement: "You don't think you are going to outrun the bear, do you?" he says. The boy on the ground looks up. "No. But I don't have to outrun it. All I have to do is outrun you."

This story is often put forward as the essence of competition. I agree, it does illustrate the essence of competition. The behavior of the boy putting on the running shoes is entirely dictated by the behavior of his companion. It is enough to outrun the other boy. That is precisely the limitation of classic competition: it is often designed to beat the other fellow—on price or quality.

There is good sense in this. If you do not beat the other fellow, you get eaten by the bear, or, in business terms, you go out of business. So I am as much in favor of classic competition as anyone else. Competition is necessary for survival. Competition, as I maintained earlier, is part of housekeeping, part of maintenance, part of ensuring the baseline. Competition is necessary for survival. Sur/petition is needed for success. That is why we need to distinguish between the two.

There is, in fact, a very simple test to illustrate the difference between competition and sur/petition. Can there be competition when there are no competitors? The answer must be that there cannot, because competition is based on comparison with others. Can there be sur/petition when there are no competitors? The answer is that there can, because you are trying to provide even better value. You try to exceed the value that you provided before. Sur/petition is value driven. You strive to sur/pass yourself.

Lumpers And Splitters

Science has been built up by lumpers and splitters. Lumpers look at things that seem very different and show that they actually have certain things in common. For example, many apparently different illnesses may all be seen as instances of autoimmune problems.

Splitters look at things that seem very similar and are often classed together, and show that they are much more different than had been assumed. For example, one type of sore throat is caused by a bacteria and can be cured with an antibiotic, but another type is caused by a virus, and antibiotics are useless.

Lumpers operate by looking at apparently different things and find a unifying factor. A lumper would achieve nothing by claiming that competition and sur/petition are the same, because they already seem similar. It is the splitter who is of value here. The splitter looks at the two and finds that the apparent similarity hides a fundamental distinction. I am trying to lay out this distinction in this book and can only hope that readers will do their own splitting.

The Same As . . .

Based on my twenty-three years of experience in the field of creative thinking, I can say without hesitation that one phrase has killed more good ideas than any other form of response. This killer phrase is "the same as. . . . "

Sometimes you come up with an idea in a group, and other members tell you that the idea is ridiculous, it will never work, it is illegal, or it is far too expensive. None of these comments are effective rejections of the idea, because you can continue to discuss the idea and show how it can be made to work, why it may not be illegal, and how it might be done in a cheaper way. Attention might then refocus on the idea.

But if someone in the group says:

"That is an excellent idea, but it is the *same as* we are now doing (or used to do)."

Such a remark is an immediate and final killer of the idea. The person making the remark acknowledges the value of the idea, but says that the idea is not worth further attention or discussion because it is already being used. There is nothing new about it. Most people have learned that this is by far the best way to get rid of an idea.

I have seen many good ideas dismissed with the "same as" remark. Usually, further examination shows that the similarity is very slight and, in fact, the idea is actually a new one. If we go to a sufficiently general level, many ideas can be said to be the same as other ideas. After all, both a horse and an airplane are just ways of getting from point A to point B. Should we have dismissed the concept of an airplane because we had the horse? The answer is that we probably would have done so. In fact, the British admiralty dismissed the idea of the wireless telegraph because they already had a way of signalling with flags!

Integrated Values

I am sure that most people in marketing will quickly claim that the concept of integrated values is the same as product differentiation, and that they have been doing it all along. I fully agree that there have been many instances of integrated values—some intentional and some accidental. I am also sure that some people in marketing do think this way. But I am equally sure that we need, very deliberately, to separate integrated values from normal marketing and product values.

The pure definition of marketing is the taking to market of goods or services. There is the choice of market, price, presentation, positioning, methods of communication, and much else.

"Here is the product, now how do we market it?"

This is too tight a definition and most marketers would reserve the right to say that products need to be altered or packaged differently in order to sell successfully. But if we enlarge the definition of marketing to include everything a corporation does in order to provide saleable value, then the definition becomes so broad that it becomes the definition of any business. We are then left without any word for "marketing" as such. We might call it "merchandising," but that is too narrow a term and deals only with things like position on shelves.

With integrated values, we seek to integrate a product into the complex value systems of the buyer. The values are neither product nor customer based. The values are based on the relationship between the customer, the product, and, most importantly, the world around them.

Bonus Bonds were set up to reward office workers who worked extra hard. Giving money as a bonus had not been very effective in the past, because people came to expect it and got upset when it was withdrawn. So there was a ratchetting upwards. Bonus Bonds were pieces of paper which only had value if used in a limited number of stores. There was no tax advantage and no special discount value. They soon became very successful. From the employer's point of view, the bonds could be given and withdrawn again and again, and were always treated as a bonus.

But why should the worker prefer to get these pieces of paper with a limited use rather than ordinary money which could be used anywhere? The answer is that ordinary money is soon lost in the salary or wage packet. There is always something which needs to be bought: a rug, running shoes for the children, a new set of tires for the car, and so forth. Bonus Bonds, on the other hand, can only be spent in stores that carry personal luxury items. So the money can only be spent on yourself, without guilt and without argument. In fact, many people who run sales organizations have come to the same conclusion. Giving money as a sales incentive may be less effective than giving vouchers for luxury items which the person would never otherwise buy.

Benefits of Focus

Those who feel that they are already thinking in terms of sur/petition and integrated values should welcome the definition of these new concepts, because such definition will emphasize and endorse their own thinking.

There is a benefit in a new word or a new concept, for it allows us to focus more directly on important matters. This is suggested in Figure 7.1. If we insist that sur/petition is

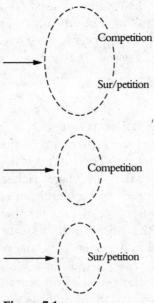

Figure 7.1

just part of competition, then we can only focus on competition and the many aspects of it which have nothing to do with sur/petition. If we develop a new concept, we can focus directly upon it.

Those who do not understand the difference between competition and sur/petition, however, will continue to claim that competition is a sufficient concept. But they will gain nothing by doing so.

8

The Three Stages of Business

There are three stages of business, though we could call them the three phases or technologies of business. Each of them covers a type of thinking and action, and views what should be done. Most simply put, the three stages are

1. Product values
2. Competitive values
3. Integrated values

Let us look at each of these in a little more detail.

The Stage of Production

It is important to produce a product or offer a service. The intrinsic value of the product or service is sufficient. The difference between having the product and going without it is a sufficient basis for business. In the early days of business, for instance, it was enough to produce a car or to offer banking and insurance services. So long as these functioned moderately well, there was a market for them. The market was also growing, so there was even room for new entrants into the market.

Thinking certainly went into getting the product produced. Thought was given to price, but not in a competitive sense. The purpose of a low price was to increase a product's market size. Henry Ford, with his famous Model T, wanted to offer a sound vehicle that was available to millions of people. As Henry Ford pioneered the assembly line, improvements in production became possible—not so much to save costs, as to increase the volume and rate of production. The market was big enough to absorb all that could be produced. Smaller companies were driven out of business or forced to join together, not by competitive pressures, but by the need for a critical size to sustain large overheads.

The stage of production is not set at one moment in time, but occurs over and over again when there is a totally new product or service line, or when a new market opens up. In time, Russia, Eastern Europe, and perhaps even China may provide these new markets. The hunger for cars in East Germany was such that even the inefficient and smelly Trabant sold in large numbers.

The Stage of Competition

In time, businesses become established and profitable. Existing businesses start to expand and newcomers are lured into what they see as lucrative markets. The simple hunger for goods becomes more or less saturated. There is still a need for goods, but now it becomes a matter of offering better quality and of persuading people to buy products.

So began the technology of competition. There was a choice of things to buy. Why should you buy one thing rather than another? Values were no longer simple product ones, but comparative competitive values: this car is cheaper than the other, goes faster than the other, or has more inside room than the other.

Production was still important, but it was now aimed at competitive values. Could the product be made at a lower price than the competitor's product—or, at least, could it be made at a similar price? Classic competition soon settled down into a matter of competing on price, quality, or product differentiation. There were those who set out to be low-cost producers (Chevrolet) and to sell in volume to a mass market. Price, with tolerable quality, was the aim. There were others (Cadillac) who aimed for premium quality and sold to buyers who could afford to pay for top quality. Product differentiation had very little real substance, but was heavily pushed by the advertising industry, which was given the task of showing why one brand was different from competing brands.

In time, product differentiation became more real. For example, the Japanese car industry gained entry to the United States when U.S. dealers told their suppliers that they did not like smaller fuel-efficient cars. After the second OPEC oil price rise in 1973, the Japanese were able to provide the smaller fuel-efficient cars which U.S. makers were reluctant to produce. The Japanese also realized that price and quality were not as mutually exclusive as some marketers had assumed. The Japanese offered low-price cars with good quality and with the many extras that American car makers had thrown out in order to reduce costs.

In the stage of competition, values are determined very largely by what one's competitors are doing. The switch from the first stage to the second is simply the switch from an empty market to a crowded one.

The Stage of Integrated Values

Most organizations are in the competition stage. Some, however, are not yet into the competition stage and still believe they are operating in the first stage of product values. Very few organizations have consciously moved on to the next stage of integrated values. Strong examples of integrated values have certainly occurred in the past, just as they are occurring in the present. But these have happened more by chance than through deliberate strategic effort.

A classic example of integrated values is the very successful French Club Méditerranée. The French do not like traveling abroad, partly because they do not speak foreign languages and partly because they believe (rightly so) that they have better standards of cooking than almost anyone else in the world. The concept of the Club Méditerranée integrated directly into these concepts: they could now go abroad, but they could take a piece of France with them. A French person would be abroad, but he or she could speak French and enjoy French cooking.

Integrated values are not simple product values or competitive values; they are values that integrate into the complex values of a customer. Nor is it just a matter of asking the customer what he or she wants. Customers may not know what they want until it has been suggested that it might be available.

The provision of integrated values may lead to a competitive advantage, but this is not its original purpose. The purpose of the original thinking is rather to achieve sur/petition through the creation of a value monopoly. Integrated values do not always lead to sur/petition, but sur/petition is always based on value monopolies. The home delivery of Domino's pizzas may be sur/petition for a while, but then it falls back to being mere competition if Pizza Hut sets up its own deliveries.

The three stages of business can be broken down as follows:

- In the first stage, attention is on the product and on production. Getting the product out there is all important.
- In the second stage, attention is on the competition. How can we do better or at least keep up?
- In the third stage, attention is on integrating into the complex values of the customer and seeking to achieve sur/petition through concept design.

Examples

We can now look at a number of different industries and try to trace these three stages.

The Auto Industry

The first stage of production is easy enough to follow, and in certain parts of the world, the first stage still persists.

The second stage of competition follows from the first stage and has been in operation for some decades. This competition is heating up at the moment because of overcapacity and the entry of Japanese and Koreans into the market. The emphasis has shifted from price to quality. The most rapidly growing segment of the market is in luxury cars, where the Japanese are challenging everyone else with products like Lexus and Infiniti.

Astonishingly, the motor industry has not yet moved into the third phase of integrated values. There are virtually no integrated values. Some cars are supposed to do something for your self-image, but this is a weak example of integrated values. Dealers are now treating clients as long–term customers instead of just making a quick sale. For example, by arrangement with IBM, every Lexus sold is tracked by computer. The current decline in car sales may finally signal to car makers that a car is no longer a lump of engineering. Unfortunately, the auto industry has traditionally been so inbred, that such new concepts may take a long time to take hold.

Airlines

The first stage of being able to fly at all was a marvelous value. Airlines indicated to passengers that they should be very grateful that they were being flown through the air. QANTAS hired stewards rather than hostesses, because it felt that classy restaurants had waiters not waitresses. Passengers, in turn, seemed very grateful. Some of that attitude still lingers today.

The stage of competition came rather late to the airline industry because of regulation. In several countries, regulation is still in force and prevents competitive pressures from lowering prices. The reasoning behind this is the need to keep national airlines solvent and operating. Competition, particularly in the United States, lowered prices on busy routes and has led to various incentives like frequent-flyer bonuses. Competition also resulted in the collapse of many airlines, and this consolidation process will doubtless continue.

The stage of integrated values has not yet arrived for airlines. There is nothing that is now being done that I would seriously regard as integrated values. Booking seats on a home computer and being able to telephone from the air are minor matters. The whole business of air travel remains clumsy, cumbersome, and highly inconvenient. Perhaps further steps await the technical development of vertical take off aircraft that can operate from city centers.

Computers

The first stage of computer production was marvelous. The difference between having a computer and not having one was huge, and industry revenues grew year after year.

Then came the stage of competition. Technology was now reliable enough for much of it to become a commodity at commodity prices. As the power went up, the costs came down. New people entered the field with highly competitive instincts. Compaq came in to challenge IBM at the lower end. At the upper end, Amdahl, Fujitsu, and Hitachi entered what had been once a monopoly for IBM. DEC focused on minicomputers and established its own niche there. Wang took the product differentiation route of the word processor. For a while, this route was highly successful, but then it petered out.

The stage of integrated values is taking place more rapidly in the computer industry than in many others. The emphasis now is on connectivity and networks. Individuals use their own desktop computers, working at home with portable computers and on the move with laptops. There is still a long way to go with integrated values, but the industry has made a good start. The next step will almost certainly be concerned with the human/screen interface of information handling. A lot needs to be done at this point—and it can be done—to make the use of information a great deal easier than it has been. Microcomputers are being integrated into different appliances. The Japanese are using fuzzy logic to offer smart washing machines that can tell the size of the load and what to do about it—without human help.

Banks

The sheer availability of a banking service was sufficient for a very long time. This is still the case in most countries in the world today. Customers plead for loans and are grateful to get them.

Then came competition, with banks on every streetcorner. There was an abundance of different offerings and different products. Credit was being marketed just like confectionery.

Today there is even more competition, because anything a bank can do can be done by other organizations as well. General Motors Acceptance Corporation is in the business of making loans. Retailers like Sears extend credit. Merrill Lynch offers investment accounts that can be used like bank accounts.

The stage of integrated values is beginning to happen with banks. Various forms of bank cards, ATM dispensers, and EFTPOS (point-of-sale fund transfers) are steps in the convenience direction. In England, the First Direct telephone bank offered by Midland Bank boasts that you can phone at three in the morning and carry out banking transactions by telephone—and you can. There is still a long way to go. Things will probably progress if the concepts are there, because banks are now coming around to the idea that their profits are going to come from ordinary customers, since business can raise its own money more cheaply.

Food Retailing

In the beginning was the street market and the corner store. Much later came the supermarket.

With the supermarket, competition started. There were loss leaders, shopping malls, hypermarkets, parking spaces, and all the rest. Once people decided to actually go somewhere to shop, as distinct from doing it in their immediate neighborhood, then competition began. Prices were cut on brand goods, but raised on fresh produce where quality could be sold at a premium. There was specialty and boutique shopping. Competitive pressures became strong.

The stage of integrated values has not happened yet. There are a few attempts to integrate shopping and leisure, as with the huge Mall in Edmonton, Canada, which draws people (even by plane) from miles around. There, you do not just go to shop, you go for a day of fun fairs, ice skating, window shopping, and eating, as well as some actual shopping. There are many possible routes of integrated values, including home shopping by telephone, shopping agents who will shop for you, video shopping, and others. The rapid growth in mail order indicates the appreciation of convenience in shopping. In the future, there will be an even greater need to segment the psychology of shoppers. For some, shopping is a real pleasure, whereas for others it is a chore.

In conclusion, in almost every industry we can easily trace the passage from the first stage of product/service values to the second stage of competition. But as we have seen, very few industries have yet begun to enter the third stage of integrated values. In some cases, there are hints and small steps in this direction. There is a long way to go, however, and a serious need for a great deal of conceptual and creative thinking. There are some classic examples of integrated value which have been around for a long time. Mail order is one of them. It came about because people living in the country simply could not get to stores and, in any case, local stores could not possibly stock a wide variety of items. As with the Sony Walkman, the concept came about for direct-product reasons, but nevertheless it achieved its success through the use of integrated values.

9

Integrated Values

Traditionally, Western manufacturers have regarded their suppliers as being on the other side of the fence—almost as enemies. There is always pressure on the suppliers to keep quality up and prices down. There is always the threat of switching to another supplier if the price or quality is not good enough. The standards of Marks and Spencer in England are so high, for example, that they insist that a single suit of clothing should be capable of being made from two pieces of cloth one mile apart on the roll.

Lately there has been a surprising change of attitude towards suppliers. This has followed the traditional Japanese attitude. In Japan, manufacturers regard suppliers as partners, and they work jointly with suppliers to improve quality. They share technical know-how instead of giving the skimpiest of specifications. All this is also beginning to happen in the United States. There is an increasing integration of the manufacturers' values with those of the suppliers.

A further integration of producers with customers has been happening over the last five years. It is not just a matter of making a quick sale and then moving on to the next sale. Motor dealers are keeping their customers on card indexes, phoning up to see how things are going, and suggesting when the next service is due. Magazine publishers have long known that it costs four times as much to get a new subscriber as to retain an old one. Customers are valuable. One of the most efficient corporations I have come across anywhere in the world is Vitro Fama in Monterrey, Mexico, a maker of glass containers. They are online by satellite to their customers and have computer programs that instantly respond to customers' needs. It is not surprising that this Mexican company has, in fact, begun to take over some American companies. So integration with both suppliers and customers is a new trend in business thinking.

Integrated values take the process a step further. By designing and offering integrated values, the producer integrates not just with the customer, but with all the complex values of the customer's lifestyle. We all live in a complex world with many values. Millions more people would buy pets if there was a good way of boarding them when leaving town.

The Swiss watch industry invented the quartz movement, but did not use the invention because it felt that this invention would kill their existing market. Anyone could use the quartz movement, whereas only the Swiss had the skills to make little cogwheels and balance springs. They were right in their thinking, as it turned out, but wrong in their strategy. Watchmakers in Japan and Hong Kong eagerly grabbed the quartz movement, and in one year the sale of Swiss watches dropped by 25 percent.

What rescued the Swiss watch industry was the very unSwiss concept of the Swatch. The sales of the Swatch at most accounted for only 2 percent of a $4 billion market, but the Swatch provided two things. First, it provided a bulk market for quartz movement so that prices could be brought down. More important, the Swatch signaled that telling time was no longer the most important thing in a watch. A $5 watch tells time every bit as well as a $30,000 watch. The Swatch was not selling time so much as fun and costume jewelry. The Swiss watch industry recovered as soon as it realized that it was not selling watches, but jewelry. Indeed, wearing an expensive watch is sometimes the only legitimate way that a man can wear, enjoy, and flaunt jewelry. And that has become the nature of the watch business today. You only have to open an in-flight magazine to find that fully 30 percent of its advertising is for very expensive watches. Telling time is only the gateway value to selling jewelry to men. This is a very clear example of integrated value, though it is an example of sur/petition only insofar as the Swiss have a reputation for watchmaking.

Many years ago, in Pakistan, a man called Nishtar took over an ailing agricultural bank. He took his loan officers out from behind their desks and put them on motorcycles. He then gave them courses in agricultural methods. His loan officers went out into the countryside to advise farmers and offer loans. At harvest time, the loan officers were out there helping to collect the harvest and making sure it was sold well. Needless to say, this excellent example of integrated value turned the bank around.

The first ATM cash dispensers in California were intended for sophisticated customers who did not have the time to stand in line in the bank. This was the initial intention, but after several months of operation it was realized that the most avid users of the machines were Mexican immigrants (some illegal) who did not speak English and and were too intimidated to go into the bank. This is an excellent example of unintended integrated value. As I have mentioned elsewhere in this book, many successful examples of integrated value were not designed or intended—they just happened.

When Mars launched the first twin candy bar there were no great expectations for this slightly different format. To their surprise, sales soared. Other makers copied with different tastes, names, and prices, and all of them did well. What was going on? At that time, people were beginning to become conscious of health, weight and diet. If you have a single bar and eat it, then that is one unit of guilt. But with a twin bar, you only intend to eat one of them. You have no intention of eating the other one right away. So that is only half a unit of guilt. Later on, somehow, you do get around to eating the remaining twin, but that is also half a unit of guilt. And as everyone knows in the mathematics of guilt, two halves do not add up to one whole.

The same concept was taken, consciously or unconsciously, by Cadbury's and used in a very successful product called "Wispa," which is a candy full of air—for which you more or less pay chocolate prices. But people are very happy to pay chocolate prices for air, because the "integrated value" is that they can eat chocolate but not feel guilty about it. Reduced fat cooking at McDonald's, fat substitutes, and oat-bran sales are all similar attempts to integrate into the concern with diet and health.

Integrated Values

Rainforest Crunch is a nut confection (there is also an ice-cream) made from nuts from the Peruvian rain forest. Produced by Cultural Survival Enterprises (CSE) which was set up by Jason Clay, it shows that rain forests can have more commerical value if they are preserved than if they are burned down. Obviously, the product integrates into the current concern for the environment in general and rain forests in particular.

A brilliant salesman once told me that when he first visited an important client, he would always make a deliberate mistake. That seems like a crazy thing to do, but the speed and willingness with which he then put right the mistake was of much greater integrated value to the client than if the salesman's performance had been faultless. He was selling a type of machinery, and of very high value to the buyer was the quality of after-sales service. The buyer was given the impression that the salesman did not want merely to make a quick sale and disappear.

A toothpaste with a large hole through the cap could offer value in several ways. In the bathroom you would be inclined to put the cap back on so that you could hang the toothpaste on a hook. Different members of the family could have different types of toothpaste, all neatly hanging up. Manufacturers might be able to dispense with packaging altogether if the toothpaste could be hung on racks.

Many years ago I suggested to Sony the value of having a business tape recorder which produced two identical tapes simultaneously. Today very few people are able to use a tape recorder at a business meeting because the other party feels at a disadvantage. But with the dual tape machine, an executive could pull out the recorder at any meeting, since at the end of the meeting a complete tape will be handed to the other party. Today there is no demand for such dual tape machines because they do not exist. I suspect that if they did exist, they would greatly increase the market for business tape recorders.

The Limits Of Competition

Today, in the United States, there is considerable overcapacity in the hotel business, and occupancy is down to 65 percent. There are many reasons for this. First, there was a tax break (abolished in 1986) which made it beneficial to invest in hotels. Many investors looked favorably on hotels because room rates could be increased from week to week as opposed to rents in office buildings, which can be locked in for years. On a classic competitive basis, there is always the hope that a new hotel will knock the older hotels out of business because the older ones are less efficient and less attractive. This has been the basis for a great deal of overcapacity in office buildings as well. It is often forgotten that older buildings have less debt and costs, and so can operate at lower prices and stay in business.

In the example of hotels, we can see an interesting clash between traditional brand image and integrated values. Traditional brand image insists that a Holiday Inn, a Hilton, a Marriott, or a Four Seasons hotel should have the nature and standards of that chain. So you look around for places which seem to need this type of hotel. The integrated value approach is to forget all about the brand image and to examine the actual needs of a neighborhood. One neighborhood might need a hotel that can take business conventions. Another might need a low-cost hotel to take families. Another neighborhood might need a hotel for business executives forced to stay downtown and in a hurry. So you integrate with the values of the place instead of insisting on brand-image uniformity. This seems to be the direction of the Tishman Realty and Construction Company, which continues to build hotels in spite of the overcapacity.

Humana operates a lucrative health insurance system that feeds patients to its own hospitals. In Japan, doctors get much of their income by selling pharmaceuticals to patients—a form of integrated value that may not be in the best interests of the patient.

There is overcapacity in food-service outlets. There are also traditional price wars, with McDonald's offering cheeseburgers for 59 cents. In recent years, much of the growth in McDonald's business has come from the breakfast trade. McDonald's persisted through years of losses in this effort at integrated values. In most European countries, breakfast is not taken at home, but on the way to work. It is a difficult market, but once established, its loyalty is likely to be high because people used to taking breakfast on the way to work are unlikely to reverse that habit. They want a simple and fast way of doing it.

In the highly competitive fruit juice area, General Foods (before it was taken over) was highly successful with the briquette package. This was just a package of a certain size. The handy size and the attached straw turned fruit juice into an instant drink. This contrasted with normal, bulkier packages of juice, which were bought as part of basic household shopping, taken home, and put in the refrigerator. In this case, a simple packaging change opened up new values.

Lockhead is not as successful as Boeing in selling airliners so it has negotiated a contract with Japanese airlines to service all their Boeing 747s. This example provides a nice contrast between traditional competition and integrated values.

Double Integration

In a painting, you normally focus upon its subject or upon the objects in it. When looking at Chinese paintings or Japanese prints, however, you also have to look at the spaces between the objects, because these are just as important.

Finding integrated values is somewhat similar to looking at the spaces in a painting. You look at the customer and at the relationships (or space) surrounding that customer. The customer is already integrated into the world. With integrated values, therefore, we seek to integrate into existing values of integration. That is why in a sense there is double integration. We seek to integrate into an existing integration.

Efficiency and integrated values sometimes seem to go in opposite directions. You can work out the most efficient number of clerks to serve at a counter. To do this, you have to measure the actual flow of customers and estimate the degree of impatience which would lead them to go elsewhere. The most efficient outcome would be the need to stand in line for a moderate amount of time. Unfortunately "average" impatience means absolutely nothing. Some people are going to get very impatient very soon. From the efficiency point of view, you could point out that to cope with these very impatient people would require an expensive number of serving clerks.

An integrated value solution would be to have one serving position with a sign indicating that there is an extra service charge of $5 at that point. Impatient people or people in a hurry might decide that it is reasonable to pay an extra charge for speed of service. If too many people decide this, then the charge could be raised.

Exactly the same principle could be applied to banks of public telephones, where one phone would have charges much higher than normal. The result is that this phone would be avoided and would therefore be available for those who need to make urgent calls and do not mind the high charge. Such people would also use the phone for as little time as possible because of the high (and unnecessary) charge.

Whenever we deal with average behavior or average consumers, we are hiding a large number of variations in personal values. As I mentioned earlier, there are several types of shoppers. The chore shopper wants to take the car to a mall on the weekend and stock up on the week's shopping. Telephone shopping, standing orders, and delivery service would suit this shopper. Then there is the pleasure shopper, for whom shopping is the best excuse to be out of the house and to meet friends. Then there are those who enjoy window shopping and are willing to expose themselves to impulse buying. All of these may not necessarily be different people, for the same person may, at different times, have different attitudes.

Market segmentation and psychographics are a help in getting at individual values, but we need to use them within the framework of integrated values. Ordinary market segmentation may show that young marrieds buy one type of car and yuppies buy another. Integrated values might seek to design a way of giving the young marrieds occasional access to the yuppie type of car and of giving the yuppie greater carrying capacity in a young marrieds type of car on the occasions when it is needed. Integrated values might work on a trade-in scheme so that the family car can be smoothly changed when the family changes.

Sadly, the British car industry has been destroyed by integrated values. Because of very high rates of personal taxation (as high as 83 percent marginal rate for many years), there was no point in giving a person a higher salary. Executives, therefore, had to be rewarded with perks, which often included the company car. At one time, up to 66 percent of British car sales were for company fleets. The corporate buyer was impressed mainly by price and was probably encouraged to buy British. The result of this integrated value phenomenon was that there was very little consumer pressure on manufacturers, who were content to churn out poor models because the fleet buyers would still buy them. The result was the virtual disappearance of the British car industry.

In the United States, 10 percent of car sales are to rental and other fleets. Each year, one million low-mileage cars are bought back and sold to dealers, who then resell them at a greater profit than new cars. As I wrote earlier, the buyers of low-mileage cars are richer and older than the buyers of new cars—in other words, discriminating buyers. The system seems to benefit everyone: the fleet owners, the dealers, and the ultimate buyers. Perhaps the sales of new cars are hurt. It seems to me that there is a lot of hidden value in low-mileage used cars, and some concept of layered ownership (first year, second year, and so on) could serve a variety of values. But if auto makers are only conscious of the need to sell new cars, then such integrated values are ignored.

Sur/petition

Integrated values do not always result in sur/petition. Sometimes it is quite easy for others to copy the integrated values so that there is no value monopoly. Integrated values can, however, give an initial advantage, which may then be maintained permanently by a good follow-through. This was the case with the Sony Walkman, but not the case with the Sony Betamax videotape system, which was pushed out of the market by VHS.

The AT&T charge card is an example of both integrated values and sur/petition, because the billing potential of AT&T and the linkage to discounts on phone calls is not easy to imitate. The Gemstar development of codes for VCR programming is also an example of sur/petition, because once the codes are generated there is no room for future alternative codes.

The Sabre reservation system set up many years ago by American airlines and said, by some, to favor bookings on that airline is an excellent example of sur/petition. Some 18,000 travel agents in the United States are hooked into that system, and even if other systems are better, the Sabre system maintains its dominant position.

After Eight chocolate mints and Avis rental cars with its slogan "we try harder," are both good and rare examples of a sort of sur/petition created by advertising. The positioning of the chocolate as one to be taken after dinner creates a unique market niche and is a mild form of integrated value. The Avis slogan is powerful because it is durable. There is no element of integrated value, except perhaps the suggestion of politeness and service.

Artificial blood is an example of a technical innovation that has suddenly been provided with integrated value by circumstance. Fear of AIDS means that blood for transfusion is often regarded with suspicion, in spite of the various screening procedures. Artificial blood is free from this fear and more convenient than autotransfusion, in which the patient's blood is given ahead of time and then reinfused during the operation. The Japanese artificial blood was used recently in a heart operation for the first time in England.

In conclusion, not all sur/petition arises from integrated values and not all integrated values lead to sur/petition, but it is likely in the future that sur/petition will depend heavily on the design of integrated values, rather than on pure product quality or image building.

10

Values And Valufacture

I travel about 250,000 miles a year by air. That is a lot of time which could be used usefully. In fact, I have written three books entirely on airplanes. The last of these (*Six Action Shoes*) was written entirely on the flight from London to Auckland, New Zealand, where I had been invited to give a speech to the meeting of the Commonwealth Law Conference. The book was written on an MC400 Psion laptop computer.

You read a lot about the excellence of laptops from Toshiba, Compaq, Sharp, and NEC. Yet the battery power of all these is a mere four hours before needing a recharge. Unfortunately, you cannot get a recharge on a 30-hour flight. Also, since you are visiting different countries, the voltages and connectors are all different. The Psion MC400, however, runs for 60 hours on a set of AA size flashlight batteries which you can replace at any hotel in any country in the world. For my purposes, the value of the Psion is vastly greater than that of the Toshiba, Compaq, NEC, or Sharp machines. For my purposes the MC400 presents unique integrated value. I am aware, however, that not many people travel as much as I do, visit so many countries, or want to write books on airplanes. So value is relative to need.

On the other hand, it is very difficult to predict value. If more people were aware of the excellence of the MC400, perhaps they might change their working habits so the need would grow. Businesses are quite astonishingly bad at predicting needs and markets. This is because they are trained only in analysis and looking backwards. If *Rocky I* has succeeded as a film (contrary to expectations), then *Rocky II, III, IV,* and *V* will be fine.

- The typewriter was only seen as an aid for blind people, because everyone else could use copper-plate handwriting.
- The market for ball-point pens was assumed to be limited to high flying aviators who could not use fountain pens because of the drop in air pressure.
- The first market calculations showed that the total world demand for computers would be limited to eight machines.
- The xerox process, which gave rise to the whole office copier industry, was only seen as an aid to printing and at one time was offered to IBM, who turned it down.
- Western Electric rejected the patents of Alexander Graham Bell which were offered to them, because the telephone was seen only as an electronic toy.

Any Western corporation supported by its market analysts would instantly have rejected Matsushita's bread-making machine as ridiculous in a culture where few people ate bread. It turned out to be perhaps the most successful product ever launched by them. It is no wonder that the Japanese trust the market more than they trust market research.

Valufacture, a new word that I have invented, is the deliberate process of creating values. The analogy is with manufacture, which is the production of things. The creation of value has been going on for a long time before invention of this word, but the new word helps to refocus attention on the deliberate creation of value.

Opportunities

American business tends to be more opportunistic than opportunity seeking. If an opportunity develops, there is usually a lot of energy directed towards jumping in with a me-too product to take advantage of the developed market. This is understandable because of the extremely short-term demands on U.S. executives. There are short-term demands from the financial markets, which want instant success. There are also short-term demands on the personal level—if you do not show instant success, you may lose your job. It is hardly surprising that American businesses are more averse to risk than those in many other countries.

The main difference between a high-class criminal and an entrepreneur is that the criminal is totally risk averse. This may seem a paradox, but it is not. The criminal does not want the risks of either investors or the market. The criminal wants everything under his or her control, and subject to the excellence of planning. A high-class criminal does not expect to be caught, and crime figures seem to justify this expectation.

The rapidly rising costs of the health-care industry ($680 billion in the United States) means that there is a strong move to curb costs and Medicare spending, which rose in 1990 by 12 percent to $108 billion. Between 65 and 80 percent of health-care costs are people costs. So there are huge opportunities for any system, method, or device that reduces the need for people. For example, Baxter International, Inc. is offering an automatically controlled intravenous drip mechanism. This would greatly save nurses' time, since otherwise they would have to be checking the drip constantly.

The DRG (Diagnosis Related Groupings) was a clever concept put forward by medical insurers to reduce the rising costs of hospitals. For every recognized diagnostic grouping, there was a standard payment for a certain number of days in the hospital. Recognized complications would be granted additional days. Instead of stretching out hospitalization to do more tests and get more revenue, hospitals now seek to get patients out as quickly as possible, because they are still paid for the standard number of days.

There is great opportunity, therefore, for value creation in the area of the containment of health-care costs.

The pharmaceutical industry is particularly fortunate in that it creates its own market. If wonder drugs keep people alive, then they get older and need still more wonder drugs. Contrast this with the unfortunate automobile tire industry, which has no choice but to kill its market. The more research that goes into tires, the longer they last. Tires that were good for 25,000 miles are now good for 40,000 miles, so the industry sells fewer tires. Nor can it raise the price of tires or hold back on research, because competitive pressures would drive companies out of business even more directly. There is a possible way out of the problem, but the industry does not seem to have spotted it.

Pollution control is going to cost the chemical industry about $4 billion. At the same time, environmental concerns are opening up huge areas for valufacture in terms of new pesticides, biodegradable materials, waste treatment, and substitutes for ozone-killing chemicals. I suggested to Du Pont that it should be relatively easy to find a coating for dinner plates so that they could be washed up without using detergents. Once this is shown to be technically possible, washing detergents might be banned because of their high phosphate production (low phosphate detergents are another opportunity area).

Baby boomers are growing up, and they want to feed their children. So there is an opportunity for mid-priced family restaurants that charge $6-7 a meal in contrast to fast food outlets at $3-4. The extra price pays for an ambience which is much more attractive for an evening out. It is worth mentioning that the classic division of the market into premium and low cost can be dangerously inadequate. There are two further markets: low cost, but with added quality; and high quality but with more affordable cost. The successful restaurants are those that start with the low cost concept and then add quality.

The dominance of commericial television networks is decreasing. In 1980 they had 80 percent of the prime-time audience. Today, this figure is down to about 60 percent. Cable television and the narrow casting it permits are opening up opportunities for more TV production. At the same time, it is difficult to see how the usual high costs of production ($1 million per hour) can ever be recouped from narrow cast use. There are opportunities here for cheaper production methods—perhaps greater use of computer graphics instead of locations.

Huge opportunities have opened up for the film industry in the video cassette area. Today this non-box office use accounts for almost 50 percent of revenue. International box office receipts have also been climbing by 20 percent a year. Costs, of course, are escalating hugely, as I mentioned earlier, so once again cost-reduction concepts are needed. Perhaps the "film factory" concepts of Hong Kong and India could be used: production lines with many films being made in parallel.

Value Drivers

Another approach to valufacture is to consider some broad value frameworks and then apply each of them to a particular situation. Many of the traditional value drivers will continue to operate effectively. There are four powerful value drivers which will become more important in the future. They are the key to the value economics that has replaced survival economics.

1. Convenience
2. Quality of life

3. Self-importance

4. Distraction

1. Convenience

You only have to look at convenience food to know that convenience has been around a long time. It will become more and more significant. Appliances will be chosen directly for their simplicity of operation. The fuzzy logic approach of the Japanese to household appliances may take hold—but only so long as it is totally reliable.

Convenience is the driver for Panasonics's AG-W1 Universal VCR, which can play PAL, NTSC and other standards of television. This means that video-cassettes from any country are directly playable. Sony's DAT (Digital Audio Tape) machine is competing with one by Philips. The Philip's machine has the added convenience that you can also play your old tapes on it.

As life gets more complex and opportunities are provided by technology, there is a thirst for simplicity and low-hassle living. Values created in this area are immediately integrated values. The well-established idea of the airline shuttle service, as, for instance, from New York to Washington, is a clear convenience value (no booking, no uncertainty). Things like car rentals and normal airline ticketing are still far too complicated.

A phone service at airports that allows you to send gifts directly is a high convenience. In Japan, there is a phone service which will apologize to other people for you. In the United

States, there is a similar service which will insult people for you. There is no end to services that offer convenience.

Finally, the concept of "asset management" is a move towards convenience. Instead of trying to follow the markets and make the right decisions, let someone else do it. This has been the essence of Swiss private banking for decades. Merrill Lynch now has $109 billion in assets under management.

2. Quality of Life

Quality of life covers concerns with health, exercise, environment, life style, family, and working habits. In the health and nutrition area, for example, it made a huge impact. The success of sports shoes (Reebok, Nike, L.A. Gear) and health equipment is only part of this. The food industry is busy churning out nutritious products for both adults and children, and developing sugar-free sweeteners and fat-free smoothers.

On the environment side, there is much concern and political action, but it is rather difficult to get individuals involved. Lead-free gasoline and recycled paper (not so profitable) are examples. Individuals are apt to be for environmental issues in the abstract, but they do not make individual choices on this basis if the inconvenience or price is high.

When workers is Europe were asked if they would like more money or more leisure time, the Germans and Swedes both opted for more time, while the British still wanted more money. The tax rates in Sweden are so high that more money means virtually nothing. The Germans, however, are prosperous and can buy all the material things they want, so a higher value to them is more time. Shorter and more flexible working hours, and part-time and cafeteria style working will all become more popular in the near future. People will want to work in pleasant surroundings. This will translate into ways of people working at home via computers and fax machines. There will be a need for strong concepts in order to translate this value framework into commercial success.

I was once asked to develop some ideas for the Swedish opposition party (now the government). The difficulty in Sweden is that 57 percent of their gross national product is taken up with government spending, which means that the majority of voters work for the government. This means that taxes are very high, and any party that sets out to reduce taxes is never going to get the votes. There is a terrible lock-in. What could the opposition party offer, for instance, to young women who worked for the government? More money would simply mean more taxes. But flexibility in working hours is a high value for anyone, particularly for women.

To some extent, there is a critical mass effect. Once enough people opt for quality of life, it suddenly becomes a necessity.

From a commercial point of view, there may be negative effects in that consumerism will suffer. People will buy cars that age well and will change them less often. People will avoid fashion clothes and buy leisure clothes they can wear for a longer time.

3. Self-Importance

The "me-generation" has been around for almost three decades now. Self-importance and self-image are powerful value drivers, as the auto industry knows very well. The designer industry and the luxury industry both know that people with money are more willing to spend it on self-image than on anything else.

If a charity ball in London is going to be attended by the Prince of Wales, a thousand tickets are sold without difficulty at £2,000 each. This is sur/petition that is unassailable. The cause is worthy. There are many other examples.

New production methods allow much shorter runs. In Japan, the concept of limited-edition cars (perhaps only 10,000 made of the type) is already in action. Further customization could mean hand-painted cars. People will come to employ exterior designers for their cars, just as they now employ interior designers for their apartments.

Napoleon was the first to realize that giving people medals and honors was much cheaper and more effective than giving them more money. This is a perfect example of integrated value. The British honor system is a continuation of that habit. People like to feel important.

You can often feel important in small groups, because you are a member of the group and others are not. This is clearly the reason for gangs in Los Angeles and elsewhere. If society does not feel you are important, then you set up a mechanism in which to feel important.

Interestingly, the growing success of cruise lines illustrates all of the drivers listed here. There is the high convenience of everything being arranged for you: hotel, meals, travel, entertainment, and so forth. The quality of life is provided by the high-quality surroundings. Self-importance is achieved by your choice of cruise line and by the social grouping you quickly achieve on board the cruise ship. The distraction element is also obvious in the entertainment.

4. Distraction

If Karl Marx were alive today, he would say that television is the opiate of the people. Marx thought that religion was the opiate, because it soothed people's pain and suffering and prevented them from rising in rebellion. Television and similar entertainments are even more of an opiate because of their addictive tendencies. If you are used to having your stimulation come in from outside, your mind never develops its own habits of thinking and reflecting. Everything is based on reacting. The more stimulation you have, the more you need to have it. The social implications of this are considerable. The commercial implications, however, mean that the entertainment and leisure industries will continue to grow.

A possible new direction for distraction is the way in which people can become entertainment for each other. The *karaoke* concept in Japan is extraordinary for two reasons. The first is that it seems so unlikely in Japan, where people are shy and inhibited (actually inhibited people often welcome a formal way of shedding inhibitions). The second reason is the simplicity of the concept in which customers pay to entertain themselves by singing at a microphone and to listen to other customers.

Types of Value

What is the value of the new house that you are thinking of buying?

- There is the actual cost.

- There is the possibility of it rising in value so that you can resell at a profit. If you buy on a rising market, you hope that it will rise forever. If you buy on a fallen market, you hope you are buying at the bottom.

- There is the location, which itself has several values: convenience to shopping malls and schools; convenience for getting to work; potential for impressing others with a classy neighborhood.

- There is the external appearance of the house, which is the image you hold in your mind—even though it matters very little when you are actually living in the house.

- There is the space and layout within the house: work space, storage space, space for the children or guests, and so on.

- There is the cost of running the house: heating, repairs, painting, and the rest.

- There is the hassle of getting a mortage, insurance, survey, and so forth.

It is a wonder that anyone can ever decide which house to buy. In the end the appeal value of a house probably wins if the financial value is acceptable.

I intend to list some types of value here. This is by no means an exhaustive list, and some of the types overlap. Other people may slice values up in a totally different way. What is important is to have a rich sense of potential values as a basis for deliberate valufacture.

Perceived Value

Perceived value is the most important value of all, because it is the main driver. Most advertising, in fact, is about perceived value. We believe that wide-eyed blonds are sweet and innocent, when they are no more so than other people. In the end, most of our thinking and behavior is based on perception.

The Japanese motor industry realizes that if an automobile looks as if it might be a snazzy sports car, then it will be bought as such by many people. It also became obvious to them that if a car looked like a macho country vehicle, people would buy it for precisely that image or perception.

There is perceived value that has no real substance, since it is the perception that is being sold.

There is perceived value that reflects a true value.

There is perceived value that reflects a true value, but one that is irrelevant to the purchaser.

Many watches are sold as being waterproof down to 100 feet. This is a real value, I suppose, and is perceived as being a significant value. Yet the number of buyers who are going to be wearing a watch at 100 feet under the surface of the sea is rather small. Similarly, the excellence of expensive claret is usually wasted on the drinker, but the perceived value is there.

Real Value

Real value means very little unless the perceived value is there. If you have occasion to use something for a length of time, you can discover its real value. Word of mouth can also spread this, but the process is slow. Even a real value reduction in price is often perceived as not being real value at all. Why, if the product is so good, is it being reduced at all?

The mother who urges her child to eat spinach rather than junk food may know something about nutrition, but the child's perceived values are different.

In the world of technical specifications, real value, of course, becomes more important—but it still has to be relevant. A computer may do a lot of wonderful things. But if you are not going to need those wonderful things, what does it matter? In this respect, the demise of the word processor is interesting. Most people use their computers only for word processing, so you would think that a dedicated word processor would make sense. What went wrong? It is true that any computer today can use a software package that turns it into a word processor. Therefore, I suspect that people felt that since the prices were similar, they might as well have the whole computer. I also suspect that the quality of the programming on word processors fell far behind. I suspect the concept will revive in a slightly different way as RFSW (Electronic Reading, Filing, Sorting and Writing).

Gateway Value

Someone from British Petroleum once told me that at that time (things were bad in the oil world), they were making more money from selling candy at the gas stations than from selling gas. I suggested that if that was the case, they should give a discount for the less gasoline that was bought. Buying one gallon, for instance, might attract a 15 percent discount. If people bought a little at a time, they would stop far more often and have much more chance to buy the profitable candy. Buying gas would then become only the gateway value.

As I mentioned earlier, timekeeping in a watch is only a gateway value to selling jewelry to men. Men will often not wear jewelry unless there is the excuse of telling time with it.

Context Value

An English-speaking person in Brazil can set up as a language teacher. There is no such value if that person is living in the United States or England. Conversely, a Brazilian in New York might set out to teach Portugese, the lambada, or the samba.

Water can be sold at a high value to thirsty people. In countries where contamination of local water is suspect, uncontaminated water can be highly priced.

Context values, like those above, can be extremely profitable. Obviously, however, context values overlap with rarity values. A painting by an obscure Dutch old master might be of little value to the owner, but of high value to the art auctioneer who knows the market.

A beautiful face in a German nightclub is of far more value on a catwalk in a Paris fashion house.

Synergy Value

All the builders of conglomerates and the energizers of takeovers talk about synergy values. The whole is greater than the sum of its parts. It is always easier to make up a story and then believe it, than to show synergy after all the parts have been brought together.

Unlike most wire-makers, Bekaert, the Belgian manufacturer, is not attached to a steel mill. This means that it can buy its steel at the best quality and prices from any source. On the other hand, Humana has found it profitable to have a health insurance company that feeds into its hospitals (as I mentioned earlier). Sony and Matsushita obviously believe there is synergy in having sources of films to feed into their downstream electronic appliances — so they took over Columbia and MCA.

Is the synergy value based on cost saving, secure supply or real combined value? Real combined value is much more rare than many believe.

Security Value

Fear of uncertainty, fear of the unknown, and fear of risk are the basis for the whole insurance business. If the price is right, security has a high value. But if the price threshold is exceeded, people suddenly become fatalistic and decide they can do without insurance.

At an ordinary level, guarantees, good service, and replacement of faulty goods do have a cost, but a much higher security value.

Wherever security values can be attached to the used-car market, there is success. Wherever security values can be attached to builders or plumbers, there is again success. Whenever the real value of the item you are buying is uncertain, then some guarantee makes a huge difference. Imagine the success of an organization that could give some security guarantee on marriage?

Appeal Value

Appeal value overlaps greatly with perceived value. Perceived value can, however, usually be defined, but appeal value may be vague and undefinable. The object just has "appeal." It may be the color, the design, or something else. There is a totality of appeal. There are appliances which sell better than rival appliances simply because they have appeal. It may be irrational and far from real or perceived values, but it works. A window shopper might say "I like that basket very much—I wonder what I could use it for?" The appeal is there, and there is a search for use. Even important functional objects like cameras may be bought simply on visual appeal and 'feel'. Designers have known this for a long time, but not too many manufacturers have been listening. The danger has been that new designs may appeal to some people, but not to others, whereas selling what has always been sold carries no surprises.

Fashion Value

Fashion values involve the artificial values of excitement and change. How do you get people to be more interested in clothes and to buy more than they need on a direct-wear basis?

The true value of gambling is not winning or losing, but paying for the enjoyment of anticipation. In the same way the true value of fashion is to make more interesting what would otherwise be very dull. Centuries ago, men were just as interested in clothing fashions as women, but today men's fashion seems dull.

There are fashions in investment as well: things to read about, talk about, and in which to be interested.

Fashion values are really interest values, but they merge into self-image values. How do I look to myself? How do I look to others? If religion does not give you reassurance, your self-image has to—but it is usually much less reliable than religion.

Function Value

Computers have to work. Mobile phones have to work. Cars have to work. Anti-missile have to work. In the end, there are function values. The difficulty is that they quickly become baseline. You expect your computer to work, so you buy it for its size appeal. You expect your mobile phone to work, so you buy it because it seems handy. You expect your car to work, so you buy it for its low price.

Function values quickly become commodity values.

In the old days when you used a computer, you had to go through the whole rigamarole of booting up, selecting from menus, and so on every time you switched the machine on. Today, we take it for granted that you come back to the exact place you were when you switched off.

New function values are powerful for a time. Then they are copied, become state of the art, and become commodity values. At the same time, new function values are high risk, because if they go wrong, they can really turn a consumer off the product. Many people have gone back from totally automatic cameras to manual ones. Others would not know how to handle a manual camera, because automatic functions have become a standard expectation.

Convenience Value

As I mentioned earlier in this section, convenience, simplicity, and reliability are becoming extremely important values. This applies especially to the service area, where existing methods are unacceptably complex. Even a simple thing like checking in to a hotel seems excessively complicated.

Yellow and Green Hats

Valufacture requires a combination of white, green, and yellow hats. The white hat is used to get general information and to give a feel for the field. Do not, however, expect information to do your thinking for you.

The green hat of creativity turns up general concepts and then goes on to specific ideas for putting these concepts into effect. There is exploration and speculation. I shall be dealing with some of the principles of creativity in the section entitled "Serious Creativity."

The yellow hat is extremely important for valufacture. The yellow hat is the "logical positive" framework. With the yellow hat we look for benefits.

Imagine a person who is almost completely paralyzed and is lying in bed able only to move one arm. What values can deliberate yellow hat thinking find here?

The person cannot move. Surely that is a bad thing. But maybe not. Today, with highly complex telecommunications networks, there is a high value of having a person at a node, someone who is always there and does not go off on holiday to the Caribbean or spend hours at lunch. You could never pay a person enough to keep him or her as immobile as the paralyzed person—and that is the high value. From the point of view of the paralyzed person, the benefits are even greater. This person can now have a full, well-paid job, can make contacts with the outer world, and also make friends.

At every moment of valufacture, there is a need to pause and ask what the benefit is, and for whom. From such pauses come hints of concepts which can then be pursued in their own right.

People and Values

There is no such thing as a value unless there are people involved. A value is something that provides benefit or opens up the possibility of benefit for someone. Values do not hang like clouds in the air. They have to be attached to people. Values require a constant asking of questions.

- Who is going to be affected by this?
- Who is going to benefit?
- Who is going to be inconvenienced?
- What will the perceptions be?
- What are the immediate effects, both short and long term?
- Will this value be noticed, will people talk about it?
- Are there any special circumstances where the value will be different?
- Are there special people for whom this could be a value?

As I suggested before with shoppers, there is a need to de-average, to look beyond the average person. An average is only an assortment of different people with different circumstances, tastes, and needs. Every teacher knows—or should know—that there is no "average" student in the class. If there are characteristics of intelligence, discipline, laziness, energy, troublemaking, or boredom, troubles at home, and so on, then a teacher knows that every possible combination of these factors will be exhibited in an individual.

The trick is to recognize individuality as a source of value, but not to end up with a market that is so small that it is of no interest to retailers. Yet there is an abundance of specialized magazines in the stores and a $100 million market for chewing tobacco.

Nature of the Values

Some values are intended. Others just happen. When customers were asked if they would use a cash-dispensing machine instead of a smiling human teller, most of the surveys showed that they hated the idea. Once the ATMs were in place, many found that they preferred to use the ATM even when there were no lines at the tellers.

We need to be quick to recognize and pick up on values which were not intended, but which simply have arisen.

Multiple Values

Your restaurant has a beautiful view of the valley. The food is superbly cooked. Food writers have written up the restaurant in glowing terms. It is fashionable to be there. You see and are seen by important people. A famous TV star lives nearby and occasionally comes for dinner. These are multiple values. All of them are a plus, but there is also a danger. The expectations of customers is so high that any fall off in standards, such as a dirty restroom, could lead to instant disappointment.

Focused Values

A small restaurant down by the wharf has built its reputation on just one dish. You go there to have chili crab. The dish is superb. Many go there specifically for this dish, but the ambience is very ordinary.

Another restaurant, with moderate food and a moderate ambience, gains a reputation for just one thing: the owner is a very outspoken character and can be very rude to the customers. In a masochistic way, some people like this, because it makes them feel important.

A cafe is known to be open all night. So if you need a meal after all other places are closed, you know where to go.

All of these examples reveal focused values that are successful.

By-Product Values

The restaurant is much frequented by financial journalists who go there to talk to each other and to pick up the current gossip. You may want to know if there is anything more to the rumor you have heard. You may even want to check out whether anyone else knows about the scoop which you think you have.

Another restaurant has a view of the entrance to a large toy store, and you want to do research, observing what sort of people go into the store at lunch time.

These examples reveal by-product values that may or may not make your restaurant a success.

Should you design for one strong value and leave it at that or should you try to build up as many parallel values as possible? The answer is not easy, because it depends very much on the field and on whether you are offering a new product or service. Certainly a multitude of weak values never add up to much. Probably the best strategy is to design for the strong values and then add other values later—as long as they do not weaken the core value. As in every other design exercise, there are things which must be there, things which must be avoided, and things that provide a special value.

Valufacture is no different from any other design process. There is a need to get to know the materials, the methods, and the clients.

11

Value Notation

I propose to put forward in this section a simple "value notation." * I believe that in the future we shall come to perceive complex information and relationships in visual patterns instead of rows of numbers. The simple mathematical graph and pie-charts are traditional steps in this direction.

The purpose of a visual notation is to give an immediate impression. Notations can also be useful for making points and for making comparisons.

We take the "V" of value and progressively enlarge it (Figure 11.1). Then we turn it on its side, facing the right-hand margin, to represent output value. We can then add an arrow to indicate the output direction, but there is no need to keep using this additional arrow.

*The notation put forward here is copyright and proprietary and may not be copied or reproduced in any book, course materials, software, electronic media or any other similar device without written permission.

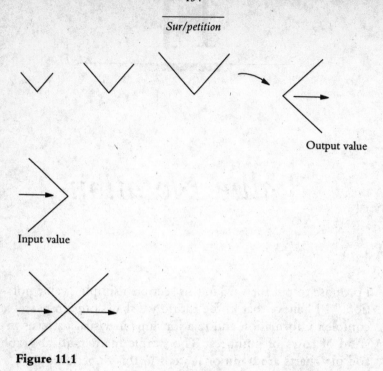

Output value

Input value

Figure 11.1

We turn a similar "V" on its side facing the left-hand margin to indicate input value. We can also indicate the input direction with a small arrow.

If we put two Vs together, we have a simple input/output system. Value is put into the system and value comes out.

Imagine that each time you wanted to cook something you had to take two twigs and rub them together to build a fire for your cooking. This could be a little inconvenient. You could have an assistant with you, of course, and the assistant could provide this fire-lighting and cooking service.

Industrial society has made life simpler by producing a cooker which can be lit with a piezo-electric spark. In this way, the cooker is providing the service that would otherwise have been provided by the above assistant. So I agree with Rosabeth Moss Kanter that all products are ways of providing a service.

So on one side, a lot of input (raw materials, steel, fabrications, paint, research, design, testing) goes into the production of a cooker. On the output side, I get the value of the cooker.

We can therefore place the cooker between the apex of the input V and the apex of the output V (Figure 11.2). There is input which has gone into producing the cooker, and there is value that comes out from the existence, function, and use of the cooker.

That is a highly simplified description of the commercial and industrial process. We can, of course, drop the cooker in future diagrams and just assume that there is a transfer point between the producer and the consumer.

But what are the values that go in on the input side? From the producer's point of view, there are costs. Money has to be used to produce the cooker. There are wages to be paid and materials to be bought. But money is not used directly. Money is a value that is used to buy other values, such as the skill and time of the workers or the oil for energy.

If a person works twice as hard for the same wages, then the input value is greater even though the money value is the same on the input side.

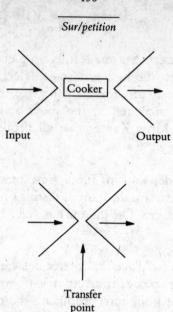

Figure 11.2

If the price of oil doubles, then the money input also doubles, but the energy-value input stays the same.

What I propose to do is to treat money values and all non-money values separately. Money values will be shown by a dotted line, and non-money values by a solid line (Figure 11.3).

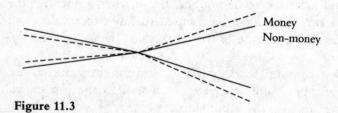

Figure 11.3

The money value on the output side represents the money the producer gets from the sale of the cooker. The value on the output side is the value of the cooker to the buyer. We can now superimpose the input/output figures for money values and non-money values, one on top of the other.

Relative sizes are shown by the width of the V as on a pie-chart. A wider V means a higher value (Figure 11.4).

If the money-value output is exactly the same as the money-value input, then there are no profits and there is no commercial business (Figure 11.5A).

If, however, the non-money-value output is greater than the non-money-value input (Figure 11.5B), then we could have the operation of a foundation which does not make money, but which can provide a greater output value than the input. If the output value is not greater, then the foundation is just getting in the way.

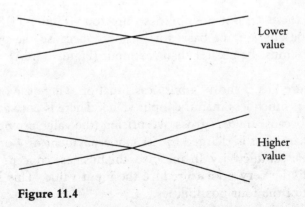

Lower value

Higher value

Figure 11.4

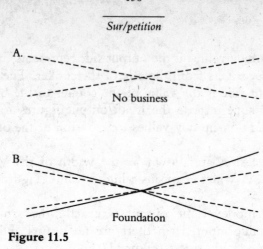

A.

No business

B.

Foundation

Figure 11.5

In the future, I shall refer to money value simply as money, and non-money value simply as value.

If we allow two sizes for the money input (big or small) and two sizes for the money output (big or small), and then do exactly the same for value input and output, we could have sixteen different combinations.

Of these sixteen possibilities only four (Figure 11.6B-E) provide any sort of basis for business, because the output money must be greater than the input (Figure 11.6A).

Figure 11.6B shows a business situation where the output value is much less than the input value. There is only a business, because there is gross overpricing (the value provided is less than what is charged for it), underpayment of workers, or great productivity. In any case, the business concept must actually be very poor to reduce the input value. This is the worst of the four possibilities.

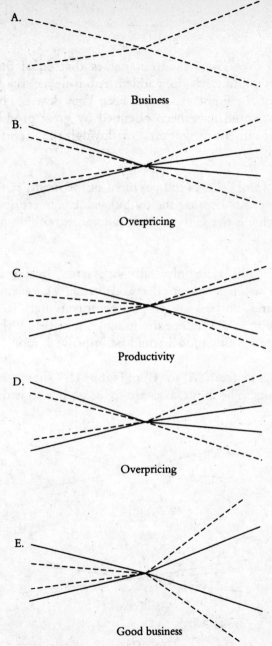

A.

Business

B.

Overpricing

C.

Productivity

D.

Overpricing

E.

Good business

Figure 11.6

Figure 11.6C shows output values that equal the input values, so nothing has been added. A business exists because the cost of the input values has been kept down. This low-cost input could have been obtained by great productivity, by underpayment of workers, or through the use of voluntary work.

Figure 11.6D shows full payment of the input, but a business only exists because the output value is overpriced. The output value is the same as the input value: nothing has been added.

Figure 11.6E is the only really satisfactory business. There is a good business concept that adds value. There is no overpricing, and workers are properly compensated. To be fair, productivity could reduce the money input below the value input, so even this model could be improved upon.

The change from (A) to (B) in Figure 11.7 shows the effect of staff cuts. The input costs are reduced, but so is the input

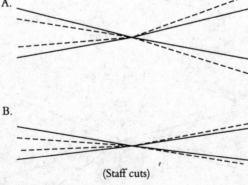

(Staff cuts)

Figure 11.7

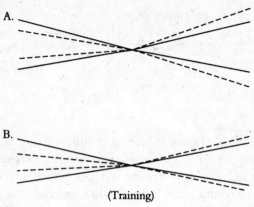

A.

B.

(Training)

Figure 11.8

value—unless there has been excess staff to begin with. The output value is also reduced, and unless there is overpricing, revenue is reduced.

The change from (A) to (B) in Figure 11.8 shows the effect of training or skills improvement. The input costs can be reduced, or the output from the same number of people can be increased along with increase of revenue.

Figure 11.9 shows what can happen in a monopoly situation. The input costs are higher than the input values because there is inefficiency. The output revenues arise from monopoly pricing that is greater than the values delivered.

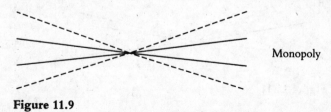

Monopoly

Figure 11.9

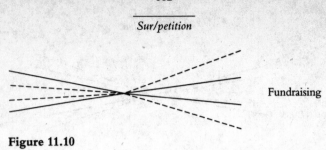

Fundraising

Figure 11.10

Figure 11.10 shows a charitable fund-raising activity. The input costs are small, because most of the input value is provided by volunteers working without payment. The output is high in revenue, but low in value, because the purpose of the exercise is simply to raise funds.

The change from (A) to (B) Figure 11.11 shows the result of a poor acquisition. The input cost (debt charges, and so on) has been raised, but the output value and revenue are unchanged.

A.

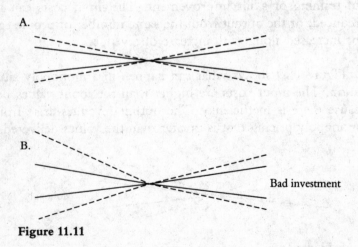

B.

Bad investment

Figure 11.11

Value Notation

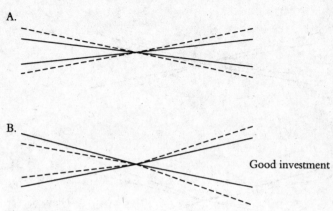

A.

B.

Good investment

Figure 11.12

Figure 11.12 shows the effect of a good investment. The input cost is raised at first, but eventually it gives an even bigger increase in input value. The output value and revenue eventually increase.

Figure 11.13 shows simple underpricing. The concept is good, so the output value is greater than the input value. Although the revenue is greater than the input cost, the price is below the values actually provided.

The change from (A) to (B) in Figure 11.14 shows the effect of a new concept. The costs stay the same, but the

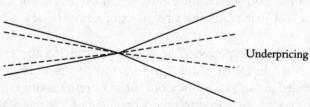

Underpricing

Figure 11.13

A.

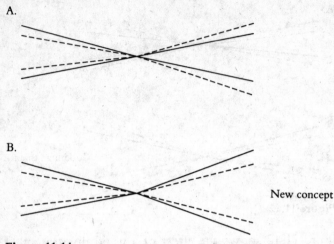

B.

New concept

Figure 11.14

output value is increased. Prices can later be increased to fit
the new values provided. In practice, any new concept is
likely to require some increase in costs. It can be seen, therefore, that a new concept is the same as any other investment.
The difference is that the cost is much less, but the risk may
be higher.

Output value may not depend solely upon input value, but
it may be helped by circumstance. You take aspirin when you
have a headache. You find the right key to free a man locked
in a room. You search for a boat when there is a flood. You
want a soft drink on a particularly hot summer day.

Figure 11.15A shows that a contribution to the output
value is made by the environment, and this is indicated by
the shaded area. The money output may remain the same or
prices may be increased to take advantage of the windfall. In
any case, the volume sales will increase.

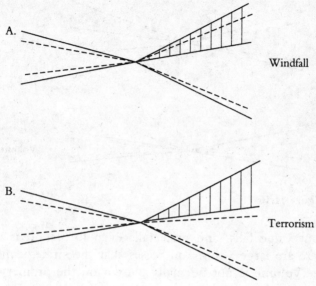

Figure 11.15

Figure 11.15B shows the reverse effect. Threats of terrorism reduce air travel by 20 percent. The airlines costs, however, are the same, but the output values are reduced. The price may not be reduced, but the volume is.

Taking the premium-quality or high-price route to competition is shown in Figure 11.16A. The input costs are high, but so is the input value. The output value is high and the price is very high because the premium level is not price sensitive, and there must also be very good margins to cover advertising and other costs.

Taking the lowest cost-producer route to competition is shown in Figure 11.16B. Input costs and quality are reduced.

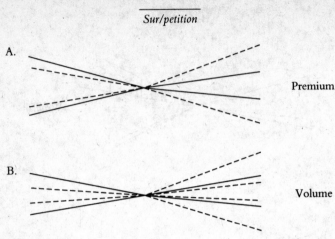

A.

Premium

B.

Volume

Figure 11.16

Output value falls, and price falls even further. It is only if there are large volume increases that the strategy makes sense. Volume is not normally shown on the ordinary input/output diagram, but is shown here with the outer dotted line on the output side (marked volume).

The total output value can split up schematically, as shown in Figure 11.17. The supposed contributions of the different elements can be indicated.

The cost or input money can also be split up into different areas, as suggested in Figure 11.18. For example, in health

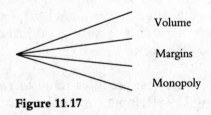

Volume

Margins

Monopoly

Figure 11.17

Value Notation

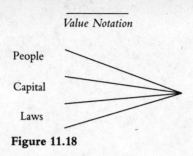

People

Capital

Laws

Figure 11.18

care, people costs can amount to 80 percent and drug costs to about 7 percent.

The value notation here indicates the changing relationships between money values (cost and revenue) and non-money values. The notation also indicates the relationship between input and output. The basic notation can be used in ways which are both simple and sophisticated. Like all notations, this one is useful for providing a framework for thinking. Points of comparison and points of attention can be picked out very easily. Changes, and hoped for changes, can be illustrated.

12

Serious Creativity

There can be no doubt that creativity is the most important human resource of all. Without creativity, there would be no progress, and we would be forever repeating the same patterns.

At a meeting of Nobel-prize laureates which I was asked to chair in 1989, only one of those present felt that he had achieved his breakthrough by systematic analysis. All the rest had had some creative insight. In hindsight, it has always been traditional to dress up these creative leaps as step-by-step logical deduction. This is necessary for communication, but it should fool no one who has studied the history of science.

If creativity is so important—and almost every corporation claims to be creative—why do we not treat it more seriously? There are several powerful reasons.

1. Every valuable creative idea must always seem logical in hindsight—otherwise, there is no way in which we

could recognize its value. So we assume that better logic would have been sufficient to get to the idea in the first place. This is totally wrong in a self-organizing, pattern-making information system. Since less than 0.1 percent of thinkers or educators have any idea of the nature and function of self-organizing information systems, most people still assume that logic must be sufficient.

2. We accept that new ideas do happen from time to time as a result of change or through an unusual coming together of circumstances. We feel that it will always be a chance process and that there is nothing we can do except wait for it to happen.

3. We accept that some people seem to be creative, while the rest are not. We believe that there is a mysterious talent for creativity which you either have or do not have, like perfect pitch in music. There is nothing a business can do except try to find and employ such creative people.

4. We have not begun to understand creativity. We haven't got a handle on it. Attempts to understand creativity by analyzing the process by which people have come to ideas is pretty useless, since it tells us nothing about the mechanism.

5. There has been a dangerously mistaken notion that the best you can do to unlock creativity is to remove inhibitions and let people be creative. This was the basis of such weak traditional methods as brainstorming. Such methods have done great damage to the development of creativity by making it seem crazy and peripheral.

6. We have believed that creativity was fine for artists, advertisers, designers, packagers, and product developers,

but that serious matters like engineering and finance require only analysis.

For all these reasons we have not treated creativity seriously. What has changed? A very great deal. We can now look at creativity in a totally new way.

1. For the first time in human history, we have begun to understand the difference between traditional passive information systems, in which information is moved about by a processor, and self-organizing, active information systems, in which information organizes itself into sequences and patterns. There is nothing mysterious about this. There are very simple ways in which nerve networks act as self-organizing systems. I suggested these ways in 1969 in my book *The Mechanism of Mind*. The ideas put forward in that book have been borrowed by many and developed independently by others. Today, they are part of mainstream thinking, and there are branches of mathematics dealing with them. Professor Muray Gell Mann (who won the Nobel prize for the discovery of the quark) once told me that my book had considered these ideas at least eight years before mathematicians had gotten around to looking at them. There is a section of my more recent book *I am right—you are wrong* which brings these ideas up to date.

Once we understand the way in which self-organizing systems create asymmetric patterns, we can then understand why every valuable creative idea must always be logical in hindsight. We can also start to design the powerful tools of creativity that we must use to move laterally across patterns. Creativity is a logical process, but it is the logic of self-organizing systems, not the traditional logic of passive systems.

2. By reference to the behavior of self-organizing systems, we can now understand why new ideas have been stimulated by chance, mistake, or accident. And we can now do something. We can set about using the process deliberately, instead of just waiting for it to happen.

3. If we do nothing about creativity, it must remain a matter of natural talent—that is obvious. Now that we have begun to understand creativity and to design specific tools, we can do something about it. We can develop creative thinking as a skill. For those who do have a natural talent (motivation, curiosity, speculation), the deliberate tools will enhance their natural skill. When I wrote my first book on creativity, I was surprised at how many truly creative people wrote to me to express appreciation and to say how useful they found the methods. For those who have never considered themselves to be creative, the creative tools open up a logical approach to creativity.

The paradox is that those who are good at playing the games that are put before them will become good at the game of creativity once it has been laid out. In fact, they might become better than the traditional rebels who have achieved creativity in the past by refusing to play the accepted games. This is why the Japanese are becoming better at creativity. In the early 1970s, the first book I published in Japan sold more copies per head than Eric Segal's *Love Story* in the United States.

4. Instead of merely analyzing the behavior of creative people, we can now look at the fundamentals of the in-

formation system of the brain and design creative tools on that basis.

5. The human brain is not designed to be creative. The brain is designed to allow incoming information to organize itself into patterns and then to use these patterns. So the traditional notion that it is enough to release inhibitions is inadequate. Releasing inhibitions will produce a mild sort of creativity. To produce serious creativity, we have to go further and to use methods which are not natural, which go against the way the brain likes to handle information. Such methods as provocation (to be discussed later in this section) are not at all natural. The traditional process of brainstorming is a little better than nothing, but it is far too weak.

6. We now know that if you have to do any thinking at all—even about the most technical matters—there is an absolute need for new concepts. The brain can only see what it is prepared to see. The analysis of information will not yield new ideas unless we have already started them in our brain through the process of creativity. It is creativity which produces the hypotheses and speculations that allow us to see things differently.

It is for all these reasons that I now prefer to use the term "serious creativity." This is to distinguish creativity based on an understanding of self-organizing information systems from creativity based on inspiration and messing around in the vague hope that something will happen. Serious creativity is concerned with laying out the logic and the game of creativity so that it is no longer a mystery. At first sight, the use of the term "serious" will seem a contradiction, because we have always thought of creativity as wacky, crazy, and off-the-wall. It is high time we moved beyond that approach, which has held back the development of deliberate creativity.

It was from the desire to bring together those corporations that were beginning to see the need for serious creativity that I set up the International Creative Forum. The charter members included IBM, Prudential, Du Pont, Merck, Nestlé, British Airways, and BAA Guiness.

The Use of Creativity in an Organization

Serious creativity within an organization needs to be used in two ways:

1. As an essential part of the general thinking skill of everyone in the organization. At shop-floor level, serious creativity is needed to make more effective such processes as quality circles, work improvement, and cost-cutting suggestions. Creativity not only provides tangible ideas, but is a great motivator, because it gets people to think about what they are doing.

    Creativity is an essential part of total-quality management and all cost-cutting exercises. Analysis can only take you so far. There is absolute need for alternatives and for new ideas. Problem-solvers have a great need for creativity, especially when the cause of the problem cannot be removed and a way forward has to be designed. Improvement depends heavily on creativity, especially the improvement of small successive steps.

    Senior management, including the chief executive, must get involved in creativity. It is not enough to delegate it to others. In my experience, it is essential for top management to understand the logic and methods of serious creativity. Creativity is simply part of thinking, and you cannot put one part aside and say that it is someone else's business.

2. Focused creativity is also needed in special areas, including strategy, research, product design, marketing, labor relations, finance, and product methods. In these areas there is a constant need for new ideas in order to solve problems or to open up opportunities. To rely solely on experience, information, and analysis is like relying on a car with only three wheels.

   It is never enough to say that there are already too many ideas. There can never be too many new ideas. And if there were, you would need to be creative about getting value from all of them.

   Sometimes people in the specialized departments that need a lot of creativity are very complacent and even arrogant. They feel they know it all and are very talented. Such arrogance is usually misplaced. Being busy is not the same as having good ideas.

   At first, engineers and scientists believe that creativity does not apply to their fields, which are controlled by facts and physical laws. But once such people see the logic of serious creativity, they realize that creativity is mathematically essential. I once gave a talk to 1200 Ph.D.'s in the research department of 3M in Minneapolis. Eight years later, a friend of mine told me that the head of research had told him that this short, ninety-minute talk had had more effect on their research than anything else they had ever done. This was because of the emphasis on the logic of serious creativity.

Does it Work?

In 1975 I gave a talk on lateral thinking to the International University of the Young Presidents Organization (YPO) in Boca Raton, Florida. The host for my talk was Peter Ueberroth. After the talk, he came up to me and told me that he had been very interested and asked me to help him do some lateral thinking for his travel company, which was called "Ask Mr. Foster."

Nine years later, someone sent me a cutting from an interview in the *Washington Post* (30 September 1984) in which the interviewer asked Mr. Ueberroth how he had managed to generate the new ideas that had made the Los Angeles Olympic Games such a success. Mr. Ueberroth replied that he had used lateral thinking, and the whole interview was about this.

In 1980, the Olympic Games nearly came to an end because no city wanted to host them because of the huge financial losses involved. At the time of writing this book, the city of Montreal has still not finished paying off the debts it incurred for the 1976 Olympics. Los Angeles only accepted the Games because Ueberroth and his team guaranteed that there would be no financial call on city funds. In the end, the 1984 Games made a profit of $225 million. Today, cities all over the world want the Games. Recently, six cities spent $70 million on promotional efforts to get the 1996 Games.

The yachting trophy, The America's Cup, has been held continuously by the United States for 150 years, except for 1983. Two years ago, at a reception in Melbourne, Australia, a person came up to me and introduced himself as John Bertrand. He said that he had been the skipper of the successful 1983 Australian challenge that had won the Cup. He told me that he felt he owed his success to the use of lateral thinking at all points, especially as applied to the innovative design of the winning boat's keel.

David Tanner of Du Pont tells how a few moments of lateral thinking led to the saving of $30 million in the development of a product. I have already mentioned how Ron Barbaro of Prudential used lateral thinking to develop the concept of "living benefits."

There are many other stories that could be told. In all such cases credit is due to the motivation and leadership of the person involved. Without such skills, nothing would have happened. It is when such talented people look around for ways of developing new concepts that they find the attitudes and techniques of lateral thinking to fit their needs.

Serious creativity requires four things:

1. Motivation
2. Attitudes
3. Focus
4. Techniques

Everyone knows that the implementation of a new idea is even more important than the idea itself. I know that, too. At this point, I am dealing with serious creativity, and I assume that an organization has a need for new ideas and is willing to implement them.

Motivation

The main difference between people who are creative and and people who are not is motivation. Call it curiosity if you like. The motivated person is willing to pause and look for alternatives. The motivated person is willing to look for alternatives beyond the obvious ones that are offered. The motivated person stops to focus on things which other people take for granted. The motivated person enjoys creative thinking almost for its own sake.

Other people need to see the need, logic, and value of creativity before they can become motivated. They also need to feel that they, themselves, can do what needs to be done.

There has to be a belief in the possibilities of creativity. Thinkers whose horizons are limited only to fixing things, often do not have the vision to imagine better or different ideas. Executives who see management as no more than maintenance regard creativity as extra hassle.

Motivation can be changed through culture changes in the organization (endorsed by senior management), through exposure to the logic of serious creativity, through training, and through structural changes that set up channels of responsibility and stimulation.

The green hat is a simple device for making time and space for creative thinking. If you ask specifically for "green hat thinking," you want to hear new ideas. Asking for green hat thinking during a meeting gives the floor to those who are trying to be creative and holds back the negative thinkers for the moment.

Serious Creativity

Attitudes

Attitudes arise partly from motivation and partly from the practice of lateral-thinking techniques.

There is the attitude of challenge.

- "How did this come to be done this way?"
- "Why do we do this?"
- "Let us look at this. Do we really need to do it?"

There is the attitude of possibility.

- "Are there any alternatives here?"
- "What other possibilities are there?"
- "What other explanation could there be?"

There is the attitude of provocation.

- "This may seem a crazy idea, but let us look at it."
- "There are some interesting points in that idea."
- "I don't like the idea, but it is a good provocation."

There is the attitude of focus.

- "Let's focus on this."
- "What are we really trying to do here?"
- "We have never looked at this before, so let's look now."

All these attitudes are based on the belief that creativity and further thinking can make a difference. They are also based on the belief that things are not necessarily being done in the best way, but only in one particular way that has evolved over time—and it could be changed.

A key part of the attitude of creativity is the willingness to make an effort. Creative effort is what really matters. If the effort is made, then results will follow—not necessarily on this occasion or on every occasion, but from time to time. The object is to try, to make an effort, to put in some thinking time.

Attitudes to creativity are very much set by the corporate culture. If the chief executive shows an interest in creativity, then much will happen. If creativity is regarded as a rather peripheral activity to be confined to the research and marketing departments, then nothing much happens.

So there are really two attitudes:

1. The attitude towards creativity on the part of senior management, other management, and individuals.
2. The creative attitude towards possibilities, work, problems, and other people.

Focus

If I ask a roomful of executives at a seminar to put down their problems, they have no difficulty in putting down five, ten, or as many as I request. As I mentioned in the section on problem-solving, executives are conscious of their problems. A problem does not need seeking out. A problem usually announces itself. It is there and must be dealt with. Many problems do need creative thinking. But there are also other creative–need areas that are not problems. These are other areas which have never been looked at (because they are not problems), but a change in idea can lead to savings or greater effectiveness.

I strongly recommend a "Creative Hit-List" as a way of making tangible the need for creativity. The Creative Hit-List is a formal list of creative–need areas. No more than half of the areas may be problems. The list is printed in in-house publications, put up on bulletin boards, and printed on postcards for people to keep in their pockets.

The Creative Hit-List can be put together from suggestions submitted by individuals and then condensed into a master list. Or a small team may be set up specifically to put together a Creative Hit-List, which is done by asking around. There may be Hit-Lists for groups, departments, or the whole organization.

The points on the Hit-List should be reasonably specific and should not be general ones such as, how do we make more profit.

There can be three types of points on the list:

1. A specific problem:
   How do we get the paint to dry more quickly?
2. A direction for improvement:
   Can we speed up the delivery of the sales information?
3. A general area need:
   Let's have some new ideas in the area of packaging.

Points on the Hit-List might get replaced by better points. Other items may be there for years without any ideas being produced. Still other items may be dropped off the list when there are enough good ideas to be followed up.

Individuals can use their creative thinking on items on the Hit-List.

Groups that are thinking about other matters may devote a few minutes from time to time to consider an item on the Hit-List.

Specific groups can be set up to think creatively about items on the Hit-List.

The Hit-List may be used in creative training, and individuals may use the Hit-List to practice their techniques of lateral thinking.

Creativity can be introduced into a department by asking the head of that department to put together a Creative Hit-List. If that person is unable to do so, then help may be offered in putting together a Creative Hit-List. Once the Hit-List is set up, enquiries can made from time to time as to what has been happening. Have any ideas been produced? What sort of efforts have been made? It is at this point that specific training in lateral thinking can be offered. The need for creativity thinking comes first, and that need is defined by the Creative Hit-List.

Although the Creative Hit-List may seem very simple, there is a high value in simply finding focus areas and defining them. Some people call this "problem-finding," but that term is misleading and only useful to contrast with solving problems that present themselves.

Once the Creative Hit-List is set up, it becomes both a challenge and an opportunity. People who want to be creative now have specified focuses. They can show their skills.

Lateral Thinking Techniques

So now we are motivated to be creative. We have the right creative attitude. We have also defined a specific creative need area: we need some new ideas right here and right now. So what do we do about it?

Let's say I am talking to a Xerox group. The focus is on the "general-area" type: We want some new ideas in the general area of convenience of copier use.

We use the random-word technique. This is the simplest of all possible creative techniques. I developed it about twenty years ago, but since then it has been copied by many people in the field, most of whom have no idea of its logical basis. I shall come to that logical basis later.

A glance at writstwatch indicates a second-hand reading of 17 seconds. This number selects word 17 from a list (frequently changed) of 60 words. The word is *nose*.

Clearly the random word *nose* has nothing whatever to do with copiers and was not selected to have any relevance. This is what provocation is all about.

Nose suggests smell. What does smell have to do with copiers? Nothing—yet. Smell is only an indicator.

Suddenly there is an idea. If the copier is not working, instead of checking lights and dials all you have to do is sniff. If, for example, you smell lavender, then the copier is out of paper. If you smell camphor, the copier is out of toner. Technically this is easy enough. Cartridges could have the different scents in small containers. When a particular circuit is activated, then the appropriate scent could be heated up and released. The cartridge could be inserted in the machine—and you could now smell what the trouble was.

The added advantage of smell as a diagnostic read-out is that you do not have to be standing at the copier. If you are working at your desk and smell lavender, then you put in more paper. The idea might be even more important for fax machines, which often run out of paper. The smell could be released as the paper is coming to an end.

The general concept is that of using smell as an indicator system. Perhaps we could use it in cars. If the car does not start, you could start sniffing!

On another occasion, the general area subject was cigarettes. The random words were *traffic light*. Within ten seconds came the idea of printing a red band on the cigarette paper at selected distances from the end. A smoker would only smoke up to the red band, so smoking would be less harmful. Smokers could select cigarettes with the band placed where they wanted it to be. With hindsight, it is fairly obvious how "traffic light" (signal, danger, stop) led to the cigarette band idea.

This technique is now widely used by a wide range of people, from product designers to rock groups seeking inspiration for a new song.

Why does it work? Logically, it is totally absurd. If a word is truly random, then it has no connection whatsoever with the focus subject. True. Therefore, any word will do for any subject. Also true. This must be nonsense. While it is nonsense in a passive-information system it is perfectly logical in a self-organizing patterning system.

Figure 12.1 shows that when you leave home, you take the usual, most-familiar road away from it. If, however, you are given a lift and are dropped on the periphery of the town, then you find your way home by using a road you would never have used when starting from home. Technically, the pattern access is different from the periphery than it is from the center. There is no mystery about that.

The mind is so good at making connections that wherever you start, you will track back and end up with one of the patterns leading into the focus area—but not the one you would have taken when working outward from the focus area.

That is why I have stressed that it is essential to understand the type of information system operating in the brain in order to understand creativity and to design simple, usable creative tools. Nothing could be more simple than the random word.

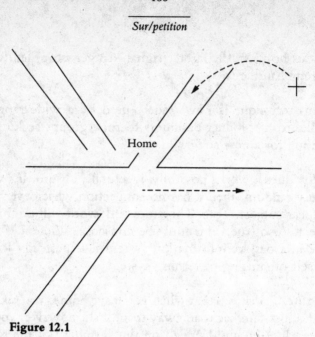

Home

Figure 12.1

Asymmetric Patterns

In a previous chapter, I used the illustration that is repeated here as Figure 12.2. Self-organizing information systems set up patterns. The patterns are necessarily nonsymmetric or asymmetric. This means that the route from A to B may be roundabout, but the route from B to A is direct. The way these patterns are set up is described in books of mine that I have already referred to, and there is no point in going over them again.

Asymmetric patterns are the basis of both humor and creativity. In both cases, we suddenly find ourselves on a side-track and immediately see the road back to the starting point

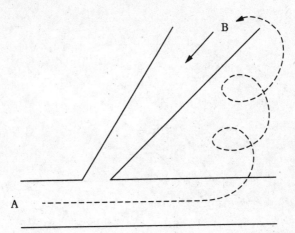

Figure 12.2

or focus. In humor, the storyteller suddenly places us on a sidetrack. In creativity, we have to find ways of doing it ourselves.

The history of science is full of examples of how chance events stimulated great ideas. There is the famous story, for example, of how Isaac Newton's idea of gravity as a force was triggered by an apple falling on his head as he sat reading under a tree.

In Figure 12.3, we can see that if we start off at the usual place, our thoughts will follow the traditional track for A towards C. If, however, we start at a totally new point N, then we might enter the sidetrack directly and then track back to A. This becomes insight or the "Eureka" moment. Suddenly we see things differently.

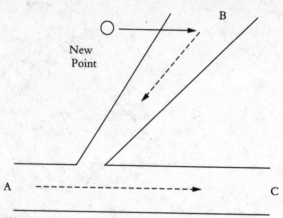

Figure 12.3

Now we can sit around under trees waiting for apples to fall on our heads, or we can deliberately shake the tree by using the formal random-word technique of lateral thinking. The random word provides the new entry point that otherwise would have to have been provided by chance.

Why do we have to rely on chance? Because if we select the new entry point, this selection will be based on our existing ideas and so will not get us to a new entry point. In certain cases, we can get a different starting point simply by directing attention from one part of the situation to another: let's start at this point. This process is also useful, but the random word has a much wider application.

Provocation

There may not be a reason for saying something until after it has been said.

That is totally contrary to normal reason, where there should be a reason before you say something.

What is the point of saying "police officers should have six eyes," or "planes should land upside down"? They seem like total nonsense statements. In fact, they are logical statements, but it is the logic of patterning systems, not the logic of traditional passive-information systems.

Figure 12.4 shows that one of the ways of getting from the main track to the sidetrack is to set up a provocation and then to use this an an intermediate position in order to move on to the sidetrack.

I invented the new word *po* to indicate a Provacative Operation. This word could never evolve in language because it is an anti-language word. It deliberately allows us to say things that we have never encountered in experience and, in

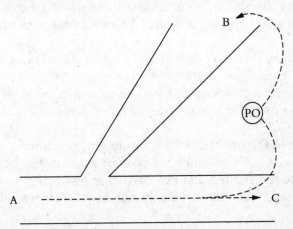

Figure 12.4

some cases, could never encounter. The word *po* acts as a protecting signal to indicate that the statement is made as a provocation.

The very valuable concept of the hypothesis allows us to speculate and invent ideas, and then look at data through these ideas. The development of science is almost entirely due to the invention of the hypothesis (which was a most useful Greek invention, in contrast to argument, which was not). A hypothesis is an idea which is not yet proved, but which we hope to prove correct. A provocation goes far beyond a hypothesis, and we make no pretence that it is correct.

In chemical synthesis and in atomic physics, if we want to change from one configuration to another, we may have to pass through an unstable intermediary before we stabilize into a new configuration. A provocation has the same effect. In self-organizing systems that always stabilize in some way, this way may be less than the best way, so there is a need for destabilization in order to settle down into a better stabilization. This point is well-known mathematically.

There are various formal and systematic ways of setting up deliberate provocations. I have described these in some of my previous books and will be paying detailed attention to these methods in a new book called *Serious Creativity*.*

One of the methods of setting up a provocation is simply to escape from something we take for granted. For example, we take for granted that taxi drivers know their way about, so we say, "Po, taxi drivers do not know their way about."

*HarperBusiness, New York, 1992.

Movement

Obviously, the process of provocation would never work if we were simply to use traditional judgment on the provocation. "Po, taxi drivers do not know their way around" would be rejected on the basis that you could not possibly run a taxi service that way.

Many approaches to creative thinking talk about delaying, suspending, or deferring judgment. Such processes are far too weak. Telling someone not to use judgment does not tell that person what to do.

We need to develop an active mental operation that we can use deliberately and specifically. I have called this mental operation "movement."

The mental operation of movement is based directly on the "water logic" of patterning systems. Movement is based on the word *to*: what does this flow to, what does this lead to? Movement is contrasted with traditional judgment, which is based on "is" and "is not." "Is this correct?" "Is this in accordance with my experience?" "Is this not going to work?"

There are five formal and systematic ways of getting movement, and these will be laid out in the book *Serious Creativity*, which is entirely devoted to the lateral thinking process. We can, however, get an idea of the process of movement by taking two of the provocations given above.

"Po, police officers have six eyes." Many years ago, one of the problems given me by the office of the mayor of New

York was a shortage of police officers. From this provocation, we moved on to the concept of increasing the eyes of the police. This led to the idea that individuals could act as extra eyes for the police. This and other ideas formed the cover story of *New York* magazine in April 1971. I believe it was the first write-up of what has subsequently become the neighborhood-watch program, which is now used in thousands of communities.

"Po, taxi drivers do not know their way about." The process of movement leads us to consider that the taxi driver might ask his passengers the way. This further leads to the concept that such taxis could indeed be used by city residents who knew their way around. This leads to a two-tier taxi system in which one type (indicated by a question mark on the roof) is reserved for residents and a normal type is available for everyone else. A taxi driver would only be able to pass from the residents' type to the general type after passing an exam on knowledge of the city.

About twenty-two years ago, I was giving a talk to the Shell Oil Company, and I suggested, as a provocation, that oil wells should be drilled horizontally instead of vertically. Today, this has become very much the new method, and horizontal wells yield four times as much as vertical wells. I even suggested at the time that the drill head would need to be powered hydraulically. In this particular case, the provocation directly became the idea. In most cases, however, the provocation only serves to take us out of existing thinking patterns in order to increase the chance of our moving laterally to new patterns.

Not Crazy

The processes I have described here are not crazy, but perferctly logical in a patterning system. They are essential in order to change perceptions rapidly. We can, of course, wait for mistake, accident, or chance to provide provocations, or we can provide them ourselves—systematically. I want to emphasize very strongly indeed that it is not just a matter of feeling free to have a crazy idea and hoping that maybe something useful will follow. That approach to creativity turns many people off. But once we can see that patterns take our thinking in one direction, then we can begin to see the logic of deliberate provocation. The specific and formal techniques will be described in full detail in the book devoted to serious creativity.

13

Concept Design

In an earlier section, I suggested that sur/petition was going to be achieved through integrated values, serious creativity, and concept research and development. This suggestion is not exclusive and does not mean that sur/petition cannot also be achieved sometimes through analysis and the use of product values.

Both integrated values and serious creativity have been considered in earlier chapters, and Concept R&D will be considered in the next section. In this chapter, however, I want to come back to concepts, since it is my belief that in the future, concepts are going to be the most important source of sur/petition and business success.

The definition of a concept that I shall use here is very simple: "A concept is a way of doing something which achieves a purpose and provides values."

Consider the Denver shoe or wheel clamp. Its purpose is to discourage drivers from parking in the wrong places in cities. The function can be described very simply: a metal clamp is placed over a wheel and prevents the use of the car until the authorities come to remove it after the parking fine is paid. This description of the concept is accurate enough, but it leaves out the key factor—inconvenience. Attempts to discourage parking by imposition of a high fine do not work well, because some drivers are quite willing to pay the fine when they are caught. But inconvenience is a much greater deterrent than a fine. You have to wait by the car until it can be released. Your schedule is wrecked, you are late for appointments, you can't go home. There is also a slight element of terror in the large yellow clamp that has attacked your car.

So we could describe the Denver shoe as a way of using inconvenience as a deterrent to irresponsible parking. That is a broader definition of the concept. We might then look around for specific ideas for other ways of putting this concept to work. The Denver shoe might be only one of them. It might be possible to lock something on to the exhaust outlet. In terms of design, we might try to improve the existing concept. The weakness of the clamping concept is that the offending car is left for a long time in a place that can block the flow of traffic. Perhaps raising the car up into the air would be an approach. How could we do that?

Level of Concept

Patent attorneys and agents are very good at describing different levels of concepts, because that is the essence of a patent application. Consider the following claims for a new game:

Concept Design

1. It is a game in which players move pieces over a playing surface.

2. (same as above but also) The playing pieces cover one or more of the marked spaces on the playing surface.

3. (same as above but also) Each of the playing pieces is asymmmetric.

4. (same as above but also) The playing pieces are L-shaped.

5. (same as above but also) The game is played on a board marked out into sixteen squares on a 4 × 4 basis.

6. (same as above but also) There are two neutral pieces that cover one square and can be moved by either player.

7. (same as above but also) The playing piece can be placed anywhere on the board provided it does not occupy the same position as before, provided that it does not overlap any other piece on the board, provided that it fits entirely onto the playing surface.

8. (same as above but also) In one version of the game, victory is achieved by denying the opponent any space onto which the opponent can move his playing piece.

We end up with a description of the L-Game, which I invented many years ago as the result of a challenge to design the simplest possible real game.

As can be seen, the description moves from the very general to a direct description of the game. From a concept point of view, levels 3 and 4 would be most useful. After that, the detail restricts the usefulness of the concept.

The Swedish film board once came to me for a session on creative thinking and for ideas on raising money for films.

In the course of the practice sessions, I put forward the following provocation: "Po, a movie ticket should cost $100."

That is a straightforward statement, but absurd as an idea. From that provocation came the specific idea that after seeing a film, a moviegoer could go back to the box office and invest $100 or more in that film. From this specific idea, we can proceed to extract the following concepts:

1. A simple way for ordinary filmgoers to invest in films.
2. A way for people to invest in films after they have seen them. This is quite different from investing before the film has been made.
3. A way for some of the initial investors to sell out at a profit at an early stage (so encouraging initial investors).
4. A way of getting moviegoers to recommend the film to others on a word-of-mouth basis. If they have invested, they will be more motivated to get others to see the film.
5. A way of using the cinema box office to collect small investments.

Each of these five concepts can be carried out with a number of different ideas. The broadest concept is the first one.

An important point in concept design is to point out differences. The special value of a concept is often pinpointed by a comparison with an existing concept. In the above example, a key point of difference is that investors can invest after the film has been made and after they have seen it and passed their own judgment as to its likely success. This is crucially different from investing up-front.

Defined Needs

Much concept design starts from defined needs.

"We need something to carry out this function."

There would be a great convenience if certain transactions could all be carried out over the telephone. For example, you could order from a catalogue by dialling in your card number, your PIN (personal identification number), and the catalogue number of the product. To some extent, this already happens today. The number might be over 30 digits long, and it is easy to make a mistake. If you use a computer screen, there is no problem. But if you do not use a screen, then the process is too fussy. There is a need for a simple device on which you can assemble the correct numbers, check them, and then send them down the phone line. That is the concept.

In this case, it is easy enough to carry through the concept by designing a hand-held device with a key pad and an LCD screen that allows you to assemble and check the numbers. The device then sends the numbers, by tone, down the phone line.

One could even imagine a catalogue-ordering system in which both products and customers had bar codes. A simple scanner could read them and transmit the requirements down a phone line.

Most security systems have a weakness because, if there is a personal code, the person holding the code can provide access under pressure to someone else. We need a way of making sure that the person giving the code is not under pressure. That is the definition of the need, and it seems quite a difficult requirement. Suppose we have a small television camera that records the pupil diameter of the guard. The average and range of the pupil diameter are then filed. Under pressure, the pupil diameter would change in size and fall outside the normal range. So the code would become inoperative. There is also no way in which the pupil size could be brought back to normal.

The Asset Base

Everything a bank does can be done by others. Cash can be dispensed by supermarkets. Credit cards are issued by AT&T, Amex, Diner's Club, and many others. Stores extend lines of credit. Loans can be obtained from GMAC or Ford Motor Credit. Businesses can raise their own money in the market or borrow from GE Capital corporation. Banks need to find new ways to make money.

The asset base may not be money or financial know-how, but people and communication channels. Banks may come to make a business out of personal financial management for their customers—by paying all accounts for a percentage charge. Banks can smooth the behavior of their customers on a sort of insurance basis. Banks can act as guarantors and bulk purchasers for clients. Banks can select groups of customers with very attractive profiles and give them special deals. Banks can act to set up joint-purchase schemes and provide intermediate holding positions when necessary. Through providing bulking, selecting, and channeling services, banks could charge permanent channel fees. As the processes became more automated, the overhead costs on all these would keep going down.

Singapore airport and Heathrow airport in London get half their revenues from the shops selling in the airport. How might one increase that revenue? The asset base is the large number of people using the airports (over 30 million a year in the case of Heathrow).

How could we give people more shopping time? Instead of people using the spare minutes before flight to shop, could they specifically come to the airport early in order to shop? Perhaps there could be a specific discount, depending on the time of the flight. If you shopped two hours before departure, you would get a 10 percent discount, if you shopped three hours before, you would get a 20 percent discount.

An overseas airport has a useful bulking asset. If you are going on holiday to a warm climate, the small town in which you live may not stock a large selection of suitable clothing because the local demand is low. But thousands of people passing through the airport have the same needs. So there would be a point in selling specific destination clothing. When a customer bought a ticket from the local travel agent, the customer would be given a catalogue of the appropriate clothing for the destination. The needed items could be reserved by telephone and then picked up before departure.

Shopping at airports is also inhibited by the difficulty of carrying bulky items away with you in order to bring them back again. There could be ways of storing items to await your return. Or items could be selected and paid for, and then delivered by mail later on. In fact, airports could provide a mail-order catalogue with photographs of items that could be selected. Specific airlines could negotiate different discounts directly for their passengers or as part of a frequent-flyer scheme.

There are many ways in which airports can use their position for sur/petition.

Concept Extraction

Any existing idea has a concept behind it. The concept may have been designed to be there, or it may have just come about. It is also possible to extract a concept that the users of the idea have not noticed.

This concept extraction applies to ideas that are already in use or to the creative process itself.

From the fast-food business, we can pick out the following concepts:

1. cheap and competitively cheap
2. good standards of hygiene and service
3. fast and convenient
4. you know what to expect
5. a meeting place for younger people
6. bulk buying of standard items

Concepts 3, 4, and 5 have been extracted and put together to give the concept of "expensive fast food." There are oyster bars and seafood bars. You know what you are going to get.

Concept Design

The service is fast and the standards high. But what you get is usually not cheap.

Tourists always complain that cafés in France seem to charge an exorbitant amount for a cup of coffee, whereas in the United States, there is a bottomless cup. Of course, what the French cafés are charging for is time. You can sit for hours at a table and only have a cup of coffee. The overhead still has to be paid, and you are occupying an expensive piece of real estate. One idea would be to charge by time. There would be a sort of parking meter in the center of each table, and you would have to feed the meter. Otherwise, it would give out a loud and embarassing whine. Your coffee could then be priced low. This is a perfectly feasible idea, and a number of concepts can be extracted from it.

1. Customers are charged not for the item consumed, but for the consumption of time and space. A separately defined table charge could also be used, and this might vary at different times of the day.
2. Customers can assess how much they wish to pay. They have control over the costs.
3. The establishment has some way of making a charge for time.
4. The establishment has a way of getting the customer to pay on an ongoing basis. Perhaps there might be a flat entry charge with a refund on leaving—depending on the time stamp.
5. There is a way of making clear what is being paid for.
6. There is a concept of charging for "human parking."

An even more practical idea would be to have a few tables with parking meters and the others without. This would ensure that some tables were always available for those who really needed a short rest or a cup of coffee.

The concept could even be developed as an attractive environment to which customers brought their own food and drink, but were charged on a time basis for the use of tables and chairs.

This last concept could then be taken and developed in another way. The customers could be made to pay not with money, but with attention. The surfaces of the tables could be video screens showing advertising for various products or services. Advertisers would do the paying.

As suggested in Figure 13.1 the creative process is always a matter of moving backwards and forwards between ideas and concepts. For this reason, it is often worth making the effort to put a concept into a practical form, because from this may arise a further concept.

Sur/petition

You have made a new film. How could you get some sur/petition advantage? You could deliberately incorporate some product and get joint advertising from the maker of that product. Television shows based on specific children's toys are a good example.

You could set up a telephone number dedicated to the film. This would automatically say something about the film and

Concept Design

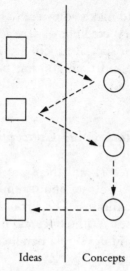

Ideas | Concepts

Figure 13.1

where and when it was showing in the neighborhood. Of course, others could catch up with that idea, so you offer to do it for competing films. In this way, you control the market and keep your film at the top (like the American airlines Sabre reservation system).

Insurance companies are very vulnerable to sur/petition. As soon as an insurer gets big enough to cater to much of the market, then a newcomer comes along, picks out one section of the market, and offers better terms. Farmer's insurance started in this way, with a company that targeted only farmers. It is always possible to establish a sur/petition position by targeting the market in this way.

If toothpastes offer to do everything possible for your teeth and gums, someone can come along with a new toothpaste that promises only to make your teeth brighter. This specific function is now very credible. There is an unending cycle between promises of special functions, adding pieces to get a broader function, and then coming back again to special functions—and so on.

Improving Concepts

If you design a concept, and there are obvious flaws in it, what do you do? Do you set about removing the faults and overcoming the weaknesses? This would be the approach of most design processes. With concepts, however, it is usually better to try again and develop a parallel concept rather than try to overcome faults.

Imagine that the *Wall Street Journal* wants to deliver a daily audio newspaper. The first idea is to have stand-alone machines into which you put your own blank cassette. Onto this is copied, rather rapidly, the audio journal that was stored on the machine and delivered down the line some while ago. The obvious problem is the time taken for this operation. This would be a particular problem, since there would be a peak demand early in the morning. A parallel concept would be to deliver cassettes to newstands and have them sell the cassettes. A problem here is the high price that companies would need to charge for the cassettes. Perhaps this could be overcome with an exchange service (bring back a previous cassette to get the new one).

Perhaps the simplest way would be to have a dedicated radio that could be switched on by a transmitted signal and which then would record the audio journal broadcast during the night. This would be simple, and you might sell the radio recorder. But then how do you get continuing revenue? Through advertising as in a normal newspaper? Perhaps a special decoding card could be bought each month and inserted into the radio to allow it to unscramble the signal.

If the concept of continuing revenue could be sorted out, then broadcast delivery during the night to any radio recorder would work. A simple timing device could set the receiver on and off at the right time. This would be the simplest design concept of all.

So now we hunt for a revenue producer—other than advertising, which might indeed work. Perhaps the broadcast message could be received on any recorder, but played back only on a special "unscrambling player" that could be rented on a yearly basis. No doubt, though, there are much better revenue concepts than this.

This excercise shows the advantage of parallel-concept approaches as distinct from trying to overcome drawbacks in the first concept you consider. We have to think in terms of alternatives, rather than polish the same gem over and over again.

14

Concept R&D

I use the term Concept R&D to make a deliberate parallel with technical R&D. The chemical industry in the United States spends $17 billion a year on technical R&D and the pharmaceutical industry spends $8.2 billion. This money is spent because corporations know that they have to spend seriously on technical research in order to stay in business.

My point is that in the future, concept development is going to be every bit as important as technical development. I might even go further to say that concept development is going to be more important. You can copy or license technology, but you need to have concepts. Even if you adopt a me-too strategy and simply wait for others to develop a concept before following with the same concept, you will need some concepts of your own to follow successfully.

As I mentioned earlier, technology is fast becoming a commodity. What is really going to matter are the application concepts. This is becoming true in the product area and has always been true in the service area, because service is directly a matter of concepts of value and concepts of organization to deliver the value.

We need to begin to recognize that concepts are as vital to business as finance, raw materials, labor, and energy. Everyone already knows this implicitly. Any business is no more than a concept at heart. It will become necessary to recognize the importance of concepts explicitly and seriously.

Good concepts, like good creative ideas, happen today as they have always happened. They come from talented individuals at a sufficiently senior level in an organization to make things happen. Sometimes corporate strategy groups take on the task of developing concepts. Sometimes advertising agencies help with product concepts, and there are specific new-product consultancies. Finally, copying is a much-used source of concept change.

The purpose of a specific Concept R&D group is to treat the development of concepts much more seriously. Such a group would not be concerned only with major strategic concepts and sur/petition, but with production concepts, communication concepts, and concepts in every area within the organization. Concepts are the organizers of information and action. We are always using concepts. When we think we are not, it just means that we are carrying on with the old and traditional concepts—often without ever being aware of their nature.

While it is perfectly true that the work of a corporate strategy group is mainly conceptual, this does not mean that it does or can do the work of the Concept R&D group. The purpose of corporate strategy is to look at the available options and at the world outside. From this base, a corporation can develop a number of possible options. One of these is chosen as a strategy. The purpose of corporate strategy is always reduction and selection for action. That is what corporate strategy should be doing—it should be concerned with action.

Concept R&D, however, has a generative or expanding function, as distinct from the reducing function of corporate strategy. Just as technical R&D opens up possibilities that are then fed into corporate strategy, so Concept R&D should also open up possibilities that are then fed into corporate strategy. Concept R&D is concerned with the possible. Corporate strategy must make a choice as to the most suitable. The two functions are synergistic. To expect the corporate strategy group to act as the Concept R&D group is to destroy its effectiveness. Corporate strategy needs to use a lot of black hat thinking and white hat thinking. Concept R&D needs to use green hat and yellow hat thinking.

Both marketing and technical R&D, or specific new product-development groups, do come up with concepts from time to time, but the focus and expertise of such groups is not directly on concepts as such. There is a difference between having a development and then looking around for a marketable use for it, and having a use concept and then looking around for the technology with which to carry it through. Technical development can indeed open up concept areas, but in the end the best results are led by concepts, not by technology. In any case, the Concept R&D group should have a free-flowing interchange of people and ideas with marketing, R&D, and product development.

The Concept R&D group should have four main functions:

1. Cataloguing
2. Generating
3. Developing
4. Testing

Cataloguing

One of the main tasks of the Concept R&D groups will be to extract, isolate, and define existing and past concepts.

Traditional Concepts

What have been the traditional concepts within the industry in general? What has been the essential nature of the industry as a whole? For example, it would be incorrect to say that the essential concept of the banking industry has been to channel funds from depositors to borrowers, because banks have taken a risk position. Channeling with channel fees has been more the function of investment banks.

Existing Concepts

What are the existing concepts within your organization? How do these differ from the traditional industry concepts? What were the conscious points of change, and how much has happened through drift or incremental change? Is everyone aware of the concepts and agreed upon them?

Historic Concepts

Are there historic concepts that are no longer in use in your organization? This need not apply only to the whole organization but also to different parts. There are times when a change in conditions may make worthwhile the revival of traditional concepts. For example, computer communication and laser cutting is making the hand-tailored suit viable again.

Dying Concepts

What are the concepts that are dying either within the industry as a whole or within your own organization? Sometimes people are conscious that a concept is dying (or suspect that it might be), but are unable to do anything about it. Perhaps the concept of large retail stores in city centers is dying. Perhaps the concept of newspapers is dying since television news is so much more up to date.

Emerging Concepts

What concepts are beginning to emerge, either in the industry as a whole or in your own organization? The concept of flexibility is beginning to emerge everywhere. The concept of joint-marketing ventures overseas is beginning to emerge in the food-processing industry. The concept of shared basic research is beginning to emerge. The concept of video-disc cataloguing is beginning to emerge.

Competitors' Concepts

What new concepts are your competitors starting to use? Are these a matter of conscious choice, or have things just evolved that way? What are the strengths of these concepts, and what are the limitations? Is it worth adopting these concepts? What modifications or improvements are possible? How much sur/petition is involved?

Indirect Competitors' Concepts

Luxury fountain pens are beginning to compete with luxury watches as ways for men to wear jewelry. In the gift area, different products compete for the gift dollar. Bottled water is a competitor for beer and wine. (Competitors do not need to be directly in the same field.) What are the new concepts that are emerging in these para-competitive fields?

Other Industries

There is a need to look broadly at other industries that are not considered competitors in any sense. There are times when some industries are forced by circumstances to move forward with a new concept faster than others. It is well worth looking to see what is happening. There may be concepts of working more closely with suppliers. There may be concepts of off-shore research or off-shore data processing. A computer company may have its software done by Indians in Bangalore through a satellite linkup. Recently an automobile consumer magazine judged the Proton Saga to be the best car out of 250 others in England in the £10,000 class. The Proton Saga is made in Malaysia, hardly a traditional auto-industry country.

The purpose of this cataloguing is to give an acute awareness of what is happening. The cataloguing can also suggest new concepts that are already in use elsewhere. The cataloging can focus attention on concepts that are dying and concepts that are emerging. The catalogue is an attempt to produce a "watch-list," just as conservation organizations produce a watch-list for endangered species.

Generating

The next task of a Concept R&D group is to generate new concepts.

The generation of new concepts may arise in three ways:

1. pinpointing specific need areas
2. perceiving needed changes and developments
3. a fresh look at existing concepts

Pinpointing

It would be the specific task of the Concept R&D group to list specific areas of concept needs. These might be bottlenecks, problems, high-cost areas, or areas of competitive disadvantage.

These targets would be collected from all different departments. They might be concept needs in production, in personnel, in communications, and elsewhere. In a sense, this is the formation of a Creative Hit-List. At the end, there is a clear sense of where concepts are urgently needed.

Changes and Developments

There may be changes in the outside world, such as a sudden rise in the price of oil, a government clampdown on medical spending, or a new environmental bill. There may be changes in the internal world, such as a new technical development from R&D or a sudden rise in costs in one area.

Such changes provide focus areas for the development of new concepts. What are the defensive concepts that are needed, and what are the opportunity concepts that take advantage of the change? There might also be concepts of procedure: how is the new technical development going to be handled?

Fresh Look

There is a high value in focusing from time to time on existing concepts or existing areas. This is not necessarily because the areas are problems or high-cost areas. You just want to focus on such areas. There is often great potential for change in areas that are not problems. Because they are not problems, they may not have been examined for a long while.

The Concept R&D group must always devote a part of its effort precisely towards a fresh look at existing concepts. Call it "concept review" or "concept reappraisal." Even the most fundamental and the successful concepts must not be immune to this review process.

Once the focus areas have been determined in the above manner, there is the need to get on with generating new concepts.

New concepts can be designed by borrowing an existing concept and modifying it.

They can also be designed through the use of information and analysis, followed by constructive thinking. The normal design process can be used.

Finally, new concepts can be designed by using serious creativity.

There is a need for training in the skills and habits of concept design. With experience, the skills build up until working in concept terms becomes automatic. The various tools, such as the tools of lateral thinking, are then used when appropriate, just as a carpenter uses whatever tools seem appropriate at the moment.

In concept generating, it is important to remember that we are not problem solving. In problem solving, we are happy with the first solution that seems to solve the problem. With concept generation, we should never be happy with the first concepts, no matter how excellent it might seem. We put the first concept to one side and proceed to develop parallel concepts, as I suggested in the section on concept design. It is never a matter of trying hard to modify a new concept so that it will work well. It is a matter of developing parallel concepts and then choosing the best one.

Concept-generating work can be done through a Concept R&D department or can be carried out elsewhere in different departments. The generation work may be carried out anywhere by individuals or by special task forces that are set up to focus on a specific concept. All this potential activity is organized, supervised, and reviewed by the Concept R&D department. There should never be a suggestion, however, that all the creative work has to be done in that department.

Concept R&D has the specific responsibility for seeing that the work gets done, but the work can be carried out in a variety of ways—including by outside consultants.

Developing

Another key task of the Concept R&D group is to develop concepts.

The concepts to be developed may have been originated as part of the generating function of the Concept R&D department, or the concepts may have originated anywhere in the organization.

The responsibility of the Concept R&D group is to take note of the new concept and to facilitate its development. This may be done by setting up contacts, by providing information, resources, and technical help, and in any other way necessary. The originators of the concepts can be encouraged to continue work on the concepts, or the concept can be taken over by the Concept R&D group and the originator incorporated into the team working on the concept.

Members of the group must be very careful not to develop the "not-invented-here" syndrome, which usually means a disdain for any new idea that has not originated within the group itself.

There comes a time when the concept is sufficiently developed to be handed over to another group such as technical R&D or marketing. The Concept R&D group should still stay involved in order to see what happens and to record the progress of the concept. If the concept fails to thrive, then it is worth noting why this has happened. The death of concepts should not pass silently.

The skills of concept development differ from the skills of concept generation in the sense that there is a steady move from the possible to the practical. Account now has to be taken of practical constraints. There is much more attention to dangers and problems. There is a need to spell out benefits very clearly and to maximize them. There is still a need for creative thinking in overcoming difficulties, but the direction has been set, and there is the need to move solidly in this direction.

The benefits offered by a concept are much more important than the novelty. Novelty is a value to the originator of the concept; benefit is the value to the user of the concept.

Testing

The way in which a concept can be tested is very much part of the concept design. It should not be a matter of designing a concept and then saying, how shall we now test this? The very design of the concept should build in the possibility of testing it. A concept that is not implemented, after all, is a wasted concept. A concept is unlikely to be implemented if it cannot be tested. That is why it is important to design a concept not only for eventual use, but also for preliminary testing. A concept that can show its benefits in preliminary testing stands a better chance of getting used than one which can not.

There are concepts which are so obvious and logical in hindsight that people want to use them right away. Cost-saving concepts can be like this: put a striking surface on one side of the matchbox instead of on two.

There are concepts which do not need investments of money, but require investments of "bother." They require people to disrupt whatever they are doing in order to try out the new concept. This can work both ways. In the famous Hawthorne effect, we find that if enthusiastic people try out the new concept, the results may be immediately more favorable than they will be later on. If a reluctant group tries out the new concept, the concept may be killed at once by poor results arising from lack of enthusiasm.

There are concepts which work well eventually, but not at first try. Drink companies know that if you give a tasting panel a number of new drinks to try, they always prefer the sweeter drinks that subsequently fail in the market. If the benefits of the concept are potentially large, therefore, it is important to insist on prolonged testing.

The design of testing involves the place, the people, and the method of measurement. Are you going to measure the savings of time, money, materials, energy, or what? How do you measure ease of working?

Quite often the testing of a concept needs to take place somewhere else—for example, in the technical R&D department or in the marketing department. Nevertheless, the Concept R&D department should keep a watch on the concept, even though the concept has now passed on to another department. If the concept fails to live up to the expectations of benefit, then a full report should be compiled by the Concept R&D group.

The design of testing procedures or situations may itself require a lot of creative thinking.

Even if a concept passes its tests and shows that it is both feasible and beneficial, this does not mean that the concept will necessarily be used. There may be other concepts that are even better. The costs and risks of change may override the benefits of the concept, or the concept may not fit with corporate strategy. The final question as to whether or not a concept is to be used ultimately passes out of the hands of the Concept R&D department.

On a strategy level, a corporate-strategy group should now consider the concepts presented by the Concept R&D group. In internal matters—for example, production—the department involved would decide whether or not to use the concept. In all cases, the history of the concept should be recorded by the Concept R&D group.

Structure

What is to be avoided at all costs is a small in-house group that feels that no one else in the organization should have ideas. That would be disastrous. The Concept R&D group is there to focus, concentrate, and supplement concept thinking throughout the organization—not to remove that function from all other areas.

The size and structure of the Concept R&D group will obviously vary with the size of the organization.

At its simplest, Concept R&D would be a person who is the nominated champion for concept development. This person would then put together a group that could serve as the Concept R&D group. They would meet periodically to carry on the functions of Concept R&D. In a small organization, all people involved would also have other line duties.

In a large organization, there should be a formal Concept R&D department. There is a value in formality since, if the grouping is informal it will only work when the members are not engaged in matters which seem (short term) more urgent. I believe that concepts are an important enough matter to merit formal attention. If concepts could be developed by computers costing $5 million, many organizations would buy them.

A small group of people would form the permanent core of the Concept R&D group. They would develop a high level of personal skill in dealing with concepts. Some would also develop training skills. The rest of the Concept R&D group would be formed from people who came into the Concept R&D group from other departments on a rotating basis. People would come from marketing, research, production HRD, etc. They would spend time working directly with the Concept R&D group. How long they spend there would depend on the size of the organization and how long they could afford to be away from their usual duties. They would bring into the group their needs and their experience. Along with people from other divisions and departments, they would work on concepts. They would eventually go back to their own duties with more experience in dealing with concepts and with perhaps some new concepts to consider further. In time, such people would set up subsidiary concept groups within their own departments.

It is not to be expected that all individuals coming in from their own departments to the Concept R&D group will be equally comfortable with concepts. At first many of them will feel awkward and even might feel it is a waste of time. But like learning to ride a bicycle, the awkwardness wears off and skill develops. This skill building and attitude changing is itself an important part of the function of the Concept R&D group.

In addition to this core group and its rotating members, there would also be other semi-permanent members of the Concept R&D group. These would be people who had shown particular talent and interest in concept development. They would be on call to take part in important discussions of the group and to take part in task forces set up to develop needed concepts. Many such people might also be involved in marketing, corporate strategy, product development, and technical R&D. But they would need to change hats when working with the Concept R&D group, not simply carry over their other functions.

So the Concept R&D group would be loose and tight at the same time. It would be tight in the sense that it had a definite existence, a definite role, and specific responsibilities. It would be loose in the sense that there would be no hard boundaries that defined who was within the group and who was not.

The People

Who should the members of the Concept R&D group be?

There is a definite need to have some senior executives involved, otherwise the group will not have sufficient status and will be treated as subordinates. Ideally the Concept R&D group should have equal status with technical R&D or marketing, even though the number of people will be fewer. If concepts are going to be treated seriously, they have to be treated seriously.

The core members of the group must be energetic, good organizers, and good at dealing with people. A lot of the work of the group in the first place will be to establish its identity and to interface with other departments without resentment. A lot of the work of the group will involve communication and liaison, so the people aspect is very important. It would be quite useless to fill the group with highly creative people who preferred to work on their own and did not get along with other people.

Although creativity is very important for the Concept R&D group, it must be remembered that much of the work of the group is not going to depend on creativity. There is also a danger with creative people that they are very judgmental of the ideas of others, and so may discourage the involvement of others in concept work.

It is more important that the members of the Concept R&D group be constructive and positive. The techniques of creativity can be learned, and the creativity of others can be encouraged.

A familiarity with concept work takes time to develop. Some people, though, find it easier than others. The core group should contain members who are adept at concept work.

Again, I would like to emphasize that the Concept R&D group is not specifically a creative group or a new-idea group. There may be old and well-known concepts that require no creativity, but become the right concepts to use. Creativity is only one of the tools that need to be used.

We treat technical R&D seriously because it requires scientists, laboratories, and machinery. Concepts only require human brains aided sometimes by computers. However, this does not mean that Concept R&D is less important. In large organizations, I would like to see at least 5 percent of the technical R&D budget spent on the Concept R&D work. In other organizations, the percentage would be of the marketing budget.

Often, concepts only work if there is a structure to support them. The serious attention that every business will have to pay to concepts in the future demands some structure like the Concept R&D group.

15

Summary

There are six key points to be taken from this book. Each key point is like a town. Around the town are the suburbs, and further out is the countryside. It is enough to keep the key point in mind—the rest will be there once you remember the key point.

Key Point 1: Housekeeping

Much of business thinking today is concerned with housekeeping. There is problem-solving, cost-control, quality management, and people care. These are all extremely important and have to be done. They are necessary, but they are not sufficient. Water is necessary for soup, but soup is more than water. When you have a competent and efficient business machine, what is it going to do?

Key Point 2: Sur/petition

Competition is necessary for survival. Competition is part of housekeeping and establishing the baseline. We need to go beyond competition (seeking together) to sur/petition (seeking above). There is a need to create value monopolies. These will be the basis of success in the future. Sur/petition is an attitude of mind, a strategy, and a matter of concept design.

Key Point 3: Integrated Values

Business has passed from the stage of product values to competitive values. The next stage is integrated values. How does the value that you offer integrate into the complex life values of the buyer or consumer? These are going to be the important values in the future. They are also the basis of sur/petition.

Key Point 4: Serious Creativity

We now know that in any self-organizing information system, like human perception, there is an absolute mathematical need for creativity. We need to move on from ineffectual methods of encouraging creativity, such as the release of inhibitions and brainstorming. We can design specific creative-thinking techniques that can be used deliberately. We can understand and lay out the game of creativity and play it (conformists can play, too).

Key Point 5: The Importance of Concepts

Technology is becoming a commodity: what matters are the application concepts. Concepts are every bit as important as finance, raw materials, labor and energy. It is not enough to rely on "me-too" copying or the haphazard use of creative intelligence. We need to take concepts very seriously indeed. Concepts are the basis of sur/petition.

Key Point 6: Concept R&D

In order to take concepts seriously there is a need for formal Concept R&D departments. These should be treated every bit as seriously as we now treat technical R&D or marketing. The concept function is not adequately handled by conventional corporate strategy.

If, in reading this book, you came to the conclusion that you knew it all already—then consider the book an endorsement of your views. But beware of the complacency of the "same as" trap.

If, however, after reading this book, you still feel that efficient housekeeping is all you need in an organization, then I think the future will prove you wrong.

Index